Before
Our
Adventures

Charles P. Hammerton

Excerpt from "No Sword School" by Alan Watts.

Printed by permission by the alanwatts.org

Back Cover Photo Credit: © by Nottingham Post October 2017

Captioned "Armed Forces award winner Charles Hammerton pictured with his pet ferret Bandit"

Edited and Formatted by Rebecka Yaeger, owner/operator of Becka's Best.

Book Cover Designed by: Kayley Kibblewhite

First Paperback Edition Printed: November 2019

Julie,

I hope you're as treasured up there

as you were down here.

Preface

For many years now, I've had an incredible bond with my pet ferret, Bandit. This book was originally going to be written about how to adventure far and wide with your pets, with some personal stories about my experiences with Bandit and why I am one of the very few people who take their ferret on amazing adventures. We've walked hundreds of miles together, been featured on TV and radio shows around the world, and most epically travelled from the arctic circle to southern Sicily in a campervan. Though our adventures together will make an interesting book, there is a back story that is first needed to be understood in order to realise why and how our adventures began.

When I speak to the public through radio, TV or on social media, I am often mistaken as a man that has always been surrounded by rainbows and butterflies. I'm often regarded as a hippy or a hipster as if being happy and independent of other people's opinions is a bad thing. Replace the '*i*' in hippy with an '*a*', and you have a description of who I am. Little do people understand what I had to go through in order to realise who I have turned up on this planet to be. To learn who I was I had to suffer abuse from awful individuals, endure my mum's death and experience a run-in or two with my own attempted suicide.

Once I had learned what I needed to, in order to realise how wonderful life truly was in all aspects, I began to wish that when I was sixteen I had a mentor or a book that would help me best understand the reason for the pain I was experiencing. While this book serves that purpose, it is impossible to hand it to my sixteen-year-old self. However, what I can do is give it to you, whoever you are, whatever your age or situation, and hope that the lessons I've learned will help you through your own struggles, or maybe even to help you realise why you struggled in the past.

This book will take you through the in's and out's of a difficult seven-year period. While I don't think the hardships I've endured are special, unique or particularly bad compared to the lives of others, I do believe that there can be a lot learned from my story that will help elevate the health and happiness of others. What I find tragic about my experience is the fact that others have similar stories that still bring them so much pain that they feel like they can never be happy again. The purpose of this book is to empower you, the reader, to learn through my past pain, so you can embrace your experiences by loving the script of your life, understanding that the hardships written into your own story have come to help you grow as an individual *if* you allow yourself to.

I'm forever grateful to the people in my life that I encountered over this period, whether I perceived them as good or bad at the time. Every soul I have met has taught me valuable lessons, whether they came from a place of love or if they wished to do me harm. Everyone who has supported me before 2017, and all the thousands of people I have met, spoken to or been in contact with since, this book couldn't have been achieved without you. I hold no grudges, regret no interactions, and wish only the very best for *all* the personas in my story.

Thank you, thank you, thank you.

Charlie

Introduction

"I always get to where I'm going by walking away from where I've been." –
Winnie the Pooh

Ants

For the most part of my life, I've been fascinated by the natural world. I can remember many times being told off in school for staring outside the window at the trees, or making my family feel sick as I bought home living creatures, ranging from the beautiful little field mouse to the gross creepy crawlies that can be found all over English woodlands under the leaf litter. I even had a fantastic time, in the military, teaching outdoor survival skills known as Bushcraft. Now, as I venture into my post-military service days, I've found a passion for teaching school-aged children the same skills, both as part of a school curriculum and through my own bushcraft company, Adventure Bandits.

This fascination I have for the abundant but simplistic beauty of nature, a world away from the domestic hustle and bustle of our modern lives, is so freely accepting of all calamities, collapses, creations and coexistences. Each creature's survival depends on another in both life and death. Even in the darkest, coldest of places, you can always find life in various forms. Powerful forces of nature can destroy large areas of habitat and disease can wipe out innumerable trees and animals, but this only creates the necessary abundance of whatever is needed for the next kingdom of creatures to reign.

I recently have learned how some species of pine trees bind their cones with such strong resin, that only the flames of a wildfire can open the impenetrable pods where the seeds reside. The Mother tree, sacrificed in the fire, allows her charred remains to release her offspring, and her ash nourishes the germination of the seedlings. And so, the circle of life and death through this evolutionary sacrifice is complete – until the next fire initiates the process again. Even the entirety of this precious planet was once a poisonous, lava engulfed void which scientists, geologists and the like believe created the perfect environment for the first early life forms to flourish. An extract from a poem I have written reflects my feelings and experience of life and death in the seasons of a woodland that I have learned through living and working in and with nature.

'Though very still and seemingly void,
life flows through this place.
Here, death is called a season,
and it surrenders to the next with grace'

A simple example of the perfect balance of nature that you can study yourself are the nests of ants. Wood ants will only build their nests on the south side of a tree where they will be given maximum hours of precious sunlight for warmth through the dense foliage. Of course, they are free to build where ever they damn well please as they do not have to adhere to council planning regulations, but to give themselves the easiest, healthiest chance of survival and a fighting chance of a long successful colonial life, they must build on the south side of a tree. Never do you see an ant contemplating whether it should build on the north side of a tree because that's what his friends are doing. Never will an ant think 'maybe I'll get around to building something better one day when the economy is right'. The ant only knows it's easiest, most fulfilling life and every day he lives it until, perhaps, little Henry comes on his summer holidays with a magnifying glass and incinerates half the colony (Henry's summer holiday, not the ants).

Of course, ants are much more simple creatures without an economy (as far as we can tell), but it makes sense to realise their existence and function in the woods of this planet are only achievable by aligning themselves with the natural flow of the sun, trees and all other subjects of the natural environment.

The natural phenomena that tells the ant the south side of a tree is the best place to build is the same invisible internal language that the acorn understands to develop deep roots and a strong trunk, the turtle to lay her eggs in rhythm with the cycle of the moon and tides and the cells within you and me to repair, replicate and repeat the process many times without our conscious input.

Between different animal species, communication has developed in its simplest of forms from electrical signals to the complex, mysterious songs of the planets most majestic of mammals, the Blue Whale. However, this mysterious 'language' without words that I'm speaking of is not one any living creature can produce through vocal cords or tangible vibrations like other forms of communication. It is unnameable, unspeakable and incomprehensible. This internal language without words that all things interpret on a subconscious level has been measured and recorded by medical professionals and scientists in the minds of humans and animals in the form of brain waves. Though the waves reverberate from areas in the brain, the command centre of living things, the invisible commander in charge of interpreting this language has yet to be discovered.

The nature of this language and the commander of the life force that is present in all living organisms, from complex brains to the nucleus of a cell, will almost certainly escape man's peering eyes forever. Scientists may try and name it, and our philosophers have tried to explain it. The poets and songwriters have at best captured its shadow through sonnets and ballads. Though once the page is turned or the song fades away, we are again left without knowing its origin or purpose and can only bask in its eternal, enigmatic, infinite wonder.

4

Civilisation has called it many different things and tried to reach an understanding of it in many ways. Along civilisation's journey of philosophical discovery, it has wrongly interpreted its purpose for the gain of the blood of a so-called enemy, control of populations and gain of gold. No matter how devastating its abuse has been, the elementary understanding of God, Krishna, Allah, Buddha, Jehovah, Tao, fate, oneness, soul, source, origin and creator all firstly evoke an overwhelming sense of peace, serenity and love to those that follow the path of its writings, teachings and philosophy. For this reason, I feel most comfortable understanding the invisible nature and connectivity of all things by calling it *the way* of things, though of course, naming something negates its true identity. It is that peaceful, divine meant-to-be or *way* of things of which I experienced intimately in my teenage and early adult life and have tied into this book. This god with a little 'g' is a constant presence in my life and everyone else's, and it unites us all, us to the nature of all things. Whether you call it Christ, Buddha or Bernard, it really makes no difference as its nameless quality, silent language and binding principle between all thoughts, things, and experiences is out of the hands of humanity. Truly, this language is present from the rhythm of breathing, to the migration of flocks of birds and the gravitational pull and movement of the Sun.

Corrr blimey! This is becoming some heavy reading! Don't worry, not everything you read in this book will be that perplexing.

This book starts with the duality between ants and trees, biology and philosophy, because it has been an important aspect of my life and is equally as important for everyone wishing to expand peace in theirs. I struggled with living a life for other people, forming my ideas based on the toxic, needy and often destructive reactions to the people I faced every day. I was totally without ease, or as one could say, *disease*. I was living day-to-day to the beat of someone else's drum, adopting the role of the victim and living with the impoverished results of that identity. Sometimes the amount of pain I was subjected to, and the constant exposure to the toxic people I chose to allow to manipulate my emotions, gave me a reason to be toxic too. I had built my metaphorical ant nest furthest from the south side of the tree as I could. Most people do not experience that mysterious language that allows a heartbeat to function without conscious input, let alone understand it. It's the same force that starts to form your complex brain just sixteen days after conception, and life and all of it's events to flow freely to our daily lives. If we try to stop it's influence, we cannot, if we try to manipulate it, we fail. To many, thoughts of lack of control are intimidating, we are conditioned to live from a state of keeping up with everyone else around us, pretending to be and forcing ourselves to be something we are not. We're constantly reminded that we are what we have, and we are what we do. So what do we become when we lose what we have, or stop doing what we do?

Unlike the fixed location of the ants and their south-facing nests, humans are destined to explore all environments and interact in harmony with people from other cultures with different languages, beliefs and philosophies, perhaps some people really do believe in an all life creating deity called Bernard! It can only be through personal experience, inspiration and beliefs that we can interpret our own individual place in the universe; the place in our circle of people we communicate with most. It is our right, no, our duty to express freely our desires and pursue our dreams in the

6

undefined course of time we have in our human bodies before we leave this place and exist as something else entirely. It is most notable that it is not our way of living that can offend other people, rather it is other people's interpretation of your way of living that all our worst critics judge. So long as our existence in civilisation (or out of civilisation, if your desire is to escape society and live in a cave) is peaceful and harmonious with the environment you find yourself in, no other person, parent or authority should lay a claim to how you should fill your years on Earth. It is with this understanding that I press the keys of my laptop as I try and convey all the lessons I have learned through trial and tribulations.

I am not a philosopher, nor am I an accomplished mental health professional. I have no qualifications, and there should be no reason for anyone to take my writing as the work of a developed and studious expert. What you should understand is that every word and sentence has come from an honest place within me and is my entire truth. Nothing I include is a Walter Mitty attempt at, as columnist Mary Schmich rightly quoted, 'fishing the past from the disposal, wiping it off, painting over the ugly parts and recycling it for more than it is worth.' I have lived, practiced and healed through these events and teachings, which I still practice and enhance every day. While some names, details and events have been altered to protect myself and the protagonists, I have adhered to my original manifesto and endeavoured to release heartfelt and genuine guidance to all those who wish to find understanding through their struggles.

I am heavily influenced by such incredible teachers as Alan Watts, Dr. Wayne Dyer and Henry David Thoreau. With this in mind, I'm confident the fundamental appreciation of Taoism brought to me through Lao Tzu, a 6th century BC Chinese philosopher (a contemporary of the more popularly known Confucius), will resonate between the letters and words within, but more importantly the teachings I have to offer. By no means should this be mistaken as a religious or spiritually evangelical book. Though spiritual themes are a prevalent part of my larger picture of life, I must profess that a god with a capital G plays no part in this story other than to demonstrate the thoughts and feelings of others. I represent and promote no religions, doctrines or beliefs other than the lessons I wish to introduce to the world as an attempt at imparting some of the wisdom I cultivated and used to keep me alive through troubling times.

Before Our Adventures is my interpretation through my experience of how life is best lived when we think of ourselves as human *beings*, and not living lives as human *doings,* or worse, humans *being done over*!

Truths and Lies

"A lie can travel halfway around the world while the truth is putting on its shoes." – Charles Spurgeon

I heaved my camera equipment and my dad's heavy, old wooden tripod up the hills and through the grassy fields some miles behind our house. It was late winter in a rural area of Essex, England. Mud clung to my boots as my equipment and rucksack dug into my back, but it wasn't much farther until I would reach my awaiting destination. It must have been just above freezing by this time in the morning, but the frozen crystals on each individual blade of grass reflected a myriad of colour across the tree-lined countryside.

I was heading to St. Andrews church, a small, ancient church in a village not far from mine. I'd selected the area as the ideal location for my photography project, not just because of the incredible vistas from on top of the hill it sat, but also because of the beautiful allure of the old English church itself. The patina of the antique stones and weathered wooden beams were perfect subjects for the photoshoot, and the low hanging winter sun added a golden brilliance to the buildings sharp edges which stood in contrast with the hazy hues of morning.

I reached the church and set up the bulky tripod, put down my rucksack and retrieved the SLR camera my sister had lent me from within. I flicked the power button across with a satisfying click but to my dismay was met with a blank screen. No battery. To add to the disappointment of my poor preparation; I had a sore back, muddy boots, and a long, heavy walk home. I had totally wasted my time.

I muttered something that rhymes with Friar Tuck and packed up my gear, ready for my disappointing trek home. Before I started back, I decided to rest and take in the gorgeous morning that had so graced my failed photoshoot.

My backside came to a thud on the bench on the east side of the church and I watched in silence as farm vehicles worked steadily miles away in a silence muffled by the acres of countryside between us. In the middle distance, the drone of commuter traffic moved ceaselessly as the night shift changed places with the day while office, retail and government workers traded their precious time for a wage. A gentle wintry breeze chilled my face, firing blood vessels and ripening my cheeks to a rosy glow. I vividly remember the sensation of the morning sunlight warming my face and the acute awareness of my surrounding environment.

For some reason that even today I still do not have an answer for, the sudden conscious understanding of how different 'Charles Hammerton' and my place in the world of rushing around, chasing ambitions was compared to my *true* nature awoke within me.

At once, a deeper understanding of the concept of who I had come to understand as 'myself' began to stir. I could somehow sense how every texture around me, every bird and tree, every movement of nature and machine, sound and temperature seemed to correlate with and complement each other. I had begun to appreciate a detachment from the symptoms of

10

the physical world interpreted as an individual and became simply the noticer (yes I did just invent a word) of the world around me and everything I could see, hear and feel.

The magnificent warmth of the sun was only so wonderful because the harshness of the cold was so bitter, just as a cool breeze on a summer day is so cooling because the heat of midday is overwhelming. Hot temperatures are only defined by cool temperatures. A long walk is only considered to be that way because of experiences with an easy, short walk. Good health could only be considered so because of our experience with poor health. Each experience I had could only be considered good or bad because of all of my other experiences together that had created my reality. Good and bad were the same thing, experienced in different ways. Creation and destruction were married together in a complex, incalculable manner. For some reason, on that winter morning, I had been drawn to that exact space and time with the intention of starting a school photography project. I would leave that idyllic hill with a gift – the primitive first step towards realising that all things, when experienced through an inner place the western world calls your spirit or soul, were perfect in whichever form they took. My consciousness had played some precise chord and the music created was an intense, inward realisation of my connectivity to everything.

The sky seemed to hum and my head ached with an uneasy understanding that my mere existence was just a tiny speck in creation's construction site, but I also had come to learn that everything, no matter how small or large, was in a constant state of evolutionary change. Even a tiny force such as a raindrop was once the ocean and eventually would become exactly that once again. I got up from my bench and started towards home, past the entrance of the church. The commonly uttered religious phrase 'God moves in mysterious ways' crossed my mind.

If creation's seemingly contradictive yet harmonious patterns were so mysterious, and God, in all the ways us humans have revered him, her or it, as a deliberate yet mysterious creator; my epiphany that morning had been intentional and undoubtedly divine. Myself, as most other British citizens, was raised a Church of England Christian in name, but apart from traditional weddings and christenings, I had never been exposed to Christianity. I was never taught Christian teachings even in school. I had no idea why I had that near-mystical, spiritual experience by the church that day, but it served as a kind of first aid box to help heal, understand and repair my emotional state of mind in the following months and ultimately years. I can only explain it as a primitive 'bigger picture' moment. In order to realise how profound this moment was for me, you must understand my complicated circumstances at this time.

***

A few months before that morning sunrise on the hill, I had become painfully wrapped up in the difficult divorce of my parents. A seemingly blissful childhood was torn apart in what I thought was one ferocious argument between my parents, though I soon discovered their marriage had been unravelling in a few collective years of dissent. I was to become another child to experience the unhealthy and all too typical adage of 'staying together for the kids'. Unfortunately, over the course of their

12

divorce, I was used as a pawn by my mother, and subsequently, I began pushing away my own father's love at arm's length.

One of them was hellbent on rescuing shameless pride, and the other tiptoed around our relationship to ensure the fragile bonds that kept us talking remained intact. I was young and had been manipulated to think hateful thoughts and even act them out. I can vividly recall a phone conversation put on loudspeaker for me to hear. I didn't know that the call had been set up so that I would be present to hear things said by a parent that no child should. I witnessed violent arguments, faked injuries, police phone calls and legal threats while events left decades in the past were dug up, cleaned off and given to me soullessly to force my position and 'side' in the pursuing conflict between my two parents.

To add to the turmoil, my hormones were flying, I had just broken up with a high school girlfriend and started college studies. My mind was occupied only with agony at discovering a large part of my life, my tight-knit, 'perfect' family had indeed for some time been smoke and mirrors. I was being forced to take sides in a miserable battle of truths and lies, blinded by rage and pushed into hateful oblivion. I greedily collected lies like they were sweets thrown from a carnival flotilla, and one time my mother gave me news of a totally fabricated event which caused me to tell my dad that I would "never talk to you again". I was in complete and utter darkness and filled with adolescent rage. Dozens of events unfolded over the six months following my parents' separation that I was both sucked into and a witness of. But all events would soon come to a climax one afternoon after coming home from college.

Tires screeched on our driveway as the Audi came to a stop at a sharp angle as if to totally block any access by car to the house. The front door burst open with such force it hit the skirting board adorning the bottom of the wall along the hallway, splitting a large gash along its length.

"Lock the doors!"

I was confused and startled to witness the sudden dramatic scene. Incoherent, angry words were coming from my mother's mouth. Gnashing curses have a distasteful sound all their own, and I had unfortunately seen this display from her many times before. However, this time it was different. On previous occasions when she would display like this I would jump to uneducated and mostly wrong conclusions and take her side against my father, but this time I knew somewhere inside me this situation should be approached with utmost caution to avoid any further conflict or mistakes. This was the first time since my 'big picture' moment that morning by the church that I had witnessed more aggressive behaviour, and something in the tone of this particular argument set it apart from all the others. I was sick of the fighting and being used as a human shield in their divorce, so I turned down the volume of the outside world and for the first time listened to my inner calm. Some guiding power from within instructed me to fall silent, simply observe the situation and refuse to be influenced by any approaching dialog. In doing this, I knew I would find the most peaceful way to be able to distinguish the truth from this situation, allowing me to act and respond as best I could to find harmony in my teenage life once again.

"Do not open the door!"

14

She barked her orders at me through a stream of tears. Running frantically about the house, she ensured all the outside doors and windows were firmly closed and locked. Her desperate, inconsolable figure then fell by the front door, clung with both hands to her telephone and began desperately to dial the emergency number. So dramatic was her reaction, it resembled the scene from Jurassic Park where the two children fight desperately to keep away the dinosaurs that stalk them through the kitchen. I half-expected to see a velociraptor menacingly peering through the small window at the top half of the door! I tried to reason with her and question what was happening and why (at that time mentioning Jurassic Park wouldn't have been a great idea, so I left that part out.)

At that moment, the all too familiar sound of my father's car, a Range Rover, was heard coming down our cul-de-sac. To my relief, and despite her hysterical reaction, the car was being driven by my father and not a dinosaur (though in 2019 he is becoming somewhat of a fossil). He parked the car to one side in the street, unable to pass the Audi roadblock, switched off the engine and hurried towards the door, not angrily, but with a concerned expression on his face. A reinforced wave of panic struck another blow to my mother and the 999 phone call was aborted before a connection was established. She moved away from the door and ran into the kitchen screaming, begging me not to let my father inside the house.

The inner, deeper part of me that had begun to emerge allowed peace to be my natural state and I simply allowed calmness to settle my nerves. I felt she was grossly overreacting, so my inner voice spoke up and made me question if she was trying to manipulate me, again. I observed my father's

15

calm attitude as he approached the large wooden front door, then, against the will of my mother, I unbolted the lock and allowed him inside.

The physical act of opening the door proved to be a great metaphor, as in doing this I had opened a door from my prison of frustration I found myself in and started to climb the ladder out of the darkness that had consumed my head and heart through the lies. My dad and I sat on the staircase and we shared quiet apologies to one another, divulging the past events that caused me to be so angry towards him and for a time not speak to him at all. The calmness I had allowed to guide me in what before would have been a manic fall out gave me clarity, and my reward for simply allowing peace into my life was our relationship restored once again.

The crazy behaviour I had witnessed from my mother had apparently been from when the two had met at a local pub that afternoon. After a conversation became heated, she had a fit of rage, stormed out the building and raced home in her car, causing chaos and nearly a traffic collision in our small village. Once I had let my dad into the house, her attitude and emotional behaviour strangely vanished. I heard the back door unlock, and she retreated to the garden, hiding away in her favourite spot, the greenhouse. Her motherly warmth towards me changed in the following days as she had felt hurt by the fact I had refused to believe her outburst was a serious cause for concern. Realising that I had called her bluff and mine and my dad's relationship had become peaceful again so quickly in one small act, she resigned herself to keeping their disputes secretive, never again including me or trying to win me over to her side of the harrowing divorce that she had fallen in love with.

The following days would see more conversations with various individuals and groups of family members, and the more I allowed the lies, half-truths and manipulations to wash out from within me, the more I saw this time for what it was. I had merely become collateral damage in a painful event that I should have been kept out of, and my reactions, feelings, and opinions on the matter were totally of my own creating. If I owned every emotion and reaction, only *I* could start to make a change to the way I had allowed events to bother me so troublesomely. The more I understood and came to terms with the fact that I had chosen myself to believe the lies I had been told instead of looking to seek the truth, the further a new feeling grew in my understanding that in order for the relationship between my father and I to grow, I had to see the relationship fragile and damaged.

The destructive dismantling of a relationship can only ever show you the worst part of what you're dissembling, for you are disconnecting yourself from that person because of what you have perceived is a bad thing. You cannot throw out the rubbish into the street while thinking, "hmm there is probably some valuable stuff in here, it's a shame I'm throwing it". You only throw away what you don't want, and you can only think of rubbish as being totally undesirable. I couldn't see the countless laughs we had, the way he raised me so well, and all the incredible moments and occasions a father and son share.

My vision had been blinded by lies, but I had judged a man by a few deeds that I had misinterpreted, and in the process negated an entire childhood of a million good things. In the dismantling process, I had replaced the true and best parts of that man with a false image I had created,

17

painted from mistruths and sprinkled with obsolete history, dug up and weaponised to the detriment of our healthy relationship. I couldn't see at that time that I hadn't just gained a bad guy of my own imaginings in my life, but I had also lost the most consistent mentor, provider and supporter in my life. It's true, 'don't it always seem to go, you don't know what you've got 'til it's gone?' Thanks, Joni Mitchell.

When I had been conned into walking down a road that separated me from truth and unity with a loved one, I had been walking away from the source of life that flows through all things. Every year millions of teenagers and young children across the world are used or encouraged by adults in a position of extreme influence in their lives to carry out harmful acts and thoughts they have towards other people. This sick tendency to hijack the admiration and respect of an innocent just to use their trust to commit a hurtful act or thought of the adults choosing brings the destructive idea of separation into their lives.

By teaching our children that thoughts of harm towards another human can be justified only results in the child growing up believing this idea as a normal reaction to not only challenging relationships but challenging circumstances. Thus, a generation of bitter, scared adults emerges, willing to blame all things on others and take no responsibility for their own actions. Any thought that has roots planted in hate and separation will bear fruit of the same hateful and separated nature. If eaten, this fruit will poison the soul. When we adopt the practice of seeing how all life and its events have happened for a reason, we make a shift from being caught up and becoming a part of what we are experiencing, to simply appreciating the undiscovered lesson it has yet to teach you. If in our time of difficulty, we can operate from a place within ourselves that doesn't look to blame, to criticise or to separate ourselves from others, we find that we can differentiate facts from opinions, the truth from lies and love from hate. To borrow a quote from one of my favourite motivators, Les Brown, "we cannot see the picture when we are in the frame".

The next time you find yourself in challenging conditions, pause and reach out for the true self you have within. If you're required to speak, speak from your heart, and always strive to end the hostility you've found yourself in. If you are in or are getting over challenging circumstances, you will see quickly that people will sense your peaceful, positive attitude and cherished relationships will heal, and the negative people in your life will be repelled by your impartial but positive attitude. The truth is only a hard pill to swallow if your mouth is full of lies.

Lessons from Truths and Lies

"You of tender years, can't know the tears that your elders grew by," –
Crosby, Stills and Nash (Teach Your Children)

Silence

The silence before any dialog is void to interpretations or differing experiences. When all around you the noise of conflict is overwhelming, be it through an argument or gossip, listen for the gaps between speaking or written text, and reach within to that consistent grounded feeling that is your true self which always remains the same at the beginning of a conversation as it does at the end of one. Between words, silence holds the same value as it did before the words. If you half silence, you'll have the same amount you started with. Double it, and it will gain no more volume. Silent contemplation is a key to allowing discovery of the truth for yourself. Never take the words of another for granted, always seek to find the wisdom in silence before accepting what someone has said as the truth or an untruth. When you do this, clarity is formed.

Today's society doesn't allow time for contemplation even in the most important of matters. A politician can be placed in front of a large audience and probed for answers over delicate subjects that require the most

20

sincere contemplations for a thorough answer to be formed. So, when statesmen and women bumble and fumble for quick answers for difficult questions, they are hounded as being idiotic or incapable of holding an office. In the ancient culture that persists throughout the aborigines of Australia, it is their custom to pause to form a well-established answer to give to a questioner. When watching certain spiritual leaders answer questions and give guidance to their devotees, they quietly sit and establish the position they will take to best advise their followers. Never do you hear "well com'on then master hurry up!", and never will a spiritual master fumble through papers and answer abruptly, batting off the supposed trivial nature of the question asked and insulting the devotee. All effort is made in silence to reach within, conjure words shaped from love and deliver them delicately, in a patient manner.

I implore you to see the gaps between dialog, even amid an argument, take rest in brief silences and find clarity through your inner peace. Remember, just as it is the gaps between the bars of a cage that holds a tiger, the gaps between words and dialog hold the key to the truth in someone's speech. No matter how bold and intimidating the words said may be, find your strength in silence. "God speaks in the silence of the heart."- Mother Teresa.

Listen

Listen diligently to the person who is speaking to you no matter how much you may already believe they are lying. Try and find the ability to hear what they have to say at a level deeper than mere words themselves. Feel the emotions of that person and try to grasp why they choose the tone they use, their foul language or hurtful phrases. Perhaps you would think it would be more beneficial to avoid the person you know to be creating vexations in your life, but I have found the opposite to be a more suitable tool for your own growth. In some cases, avoiding the person can be more detrimental to forming a thorough picture of why they are engaged in such destructive dialog with you or someone else. I lived with my mother and could see how terribly painful this divorce was for her. Whether or not her pain was worsened by her egotism or prideful nature, the pain was real, and the manner in which she argued, debated and conversed was the best way she knew how to behave at the time. If I was to completely avoid her and sever our relationship by heaving my emotions and love away from her to transfer it to my father, I would have regained my father-son bond, but lost my ties to my mother.

Instead of impatiently waiting to take turns in a conversation or argument, suspend your ego until the person you're speaking with has finished. If they raise a point on the contrary to yours, again remind yourself to listen tentatively. Ask them more questions about their point and seek to clarify what they have said before you attempt to counter them. You may find that they simply run out of words to say or even realise themselves that what they are saying isn't true, justifiable or reasonable and end the quarrel. Listening to a person's argument thoroughly isn't a way of allowing your opinions to be subordinate to theirs, but a way of thoroughly understanding the passionate opinions of others so that if you do find it necessary to explain your opinion or reasoning, you speak to them with care and compassion so as not to create further tension. The only reason you should want to be the benefactor of a debate is you believe your way is the best to go forward with. If you start going forward with your preferred views and opinions, which you feel are justified, from a stubborn, uncompassionate position the intention of your best thoughts have already been completely undermined.

Listening to a critic and truly valuing their opinion doesn't mean you have to accept it as your own, but allows you to take the perspective of the person in question so you can better sympathise with that individual. Every liar and saboteur of the truth has a lesson to teach you, no matter how painful or brutish there hindrance to you has become.

Love

The opinion of whether the world, life or people are largely good or bad has been masterfully put to question by everyone's favourite eccentric scientist, Albert Einstein. Famously Einstein asked the question, "do you think this is a friendly or unfriendly universe?" Any person or event can keep you in a negative position all your life or be looked at as an opportunity to grow. I don't suppose you can be jumping for joy when your partner has cheated on you and lied to your face for many months, but it goes without saying that what doesn't kill you makes you stronger (so long as you take time to heal and unbox the truth appropriately and don't just cover it up, otherwise what doesn't kill you will give you anxiety and trust issues). When we explore Einstein's question and imagine the world as an unfriendly place, love is left clinging for existence and destruction becomes the only driving force of life. But of course, for life to go on, we must have creation, which is the very essence of what love is. If more bad rather than good acts had existed, by now love would be exhausted and would have succumbed to the darkness. Even in the heat of conflict, famine and killing, good deeds seem to outshine the darkest of times. It is by this standard that I believe mankind has come to accept love and kindness as the underpinning current of what makes life worth living, even through the most dreadful of times.

When your silence unscrambles the words you're hearing and you start to listen sympathetically to a person causing you mischief, find the place within yourself to operate from that is only loving and only wishes to be loved. Like a parent who humours a child's fantasy or exaggerated claim, you must do the same with your identified liar. This isn't to say you should mock or scorn them, or even make out in any way that you're dissatisfied with their opinion, its simply to handle their comment in the most passive, considerate way possible. This keeps your mind in a state of peace while showing your challenger that you've received their information, recognised it, but haven't confirmed whether or not you've agreed with them. They will then either not engage you again on this topic or they may feel compelled to challenge your position, only making them appear forceful. This forcefulness destroys honesty and truth, as the truth once fully exposed needs no forceful explanation.

Keeping an open, loving mind to whatever point or opinions are made against you or another can also be a great way of observing how lovingly you are acting too. As I have previously mentioned, I did not act in a good way sometimes when I went through my ordeal with my mother and father. Being open, loving and independent of the anxiety that another person is trying to conjure out of you allows you to really see that perhaps your intolerance of another person is hindering your ability to see your own actions. Loving the soul and essence of that person, appreciating their words and deciphering what is un-aimed anger compared to a genuine concern about how your actions are harming others can only benefit yourself on the road to becoming a better person. Changing the way you may be acting also helps to calm the nerves of your accuser and has the potential to show them your willingness to accept and change behaviour, encouraging them to do the same. If your only response is to turn away from everything they are saying, or find the fault in them when they accuse you of some wrongdoing that you may be liable for, you will appear more arrogant and that can be like a red flag to a bull.

The Tao Te Cheng, a Chinese book of principles written thousands of years ago states, "what is a good man but a bad man's teacher? What is a bad man, but a good man's job?" Here Lau Tzu, the writer of the Tao, is encouraging us to remember that good deeds teach wrongdoers the errors of their ways, and a 'bad man' will always be the occupation of a good man to teach and realign his thinking and place love in every part of his life. The alternative to not learning valuable lessons from difficult people or situations would be to call your difficulties a pointless stumbling block on the futile road of life– if you haven't guessed by now, this book isn't issuing any negativity!

Spite and Kindness

"Circumstances don't make the man; they reveal him." – *Epictetus*

The dust of life settled and the water began to clear after I started to illuminate the truth in my world. I still lived with lies being spread about myself and other close family members, and hateful feelings surrounded me, but I now knew I was free to fix my attention on good thoughts, enjoy the most loving feelings around me and wish the best for those trying to disable my happy attitude. It was during this time that the most important step in my independence as a young man materialised as I realise that college didn't fit my agenda. I disagreed with the way I was just being force-fed information to prepare me for a university that I knew I didn't want to go to, just to live a life in a profession or occupation that I know wasn't the root of how life should be experienced to the fullest. Why should our young people be taught so early on in their lives that the only way to succeed is to reach a high echelon of society through hours of linear study, mundane work for corporate gain and live a six-day on, one day off life-style? I align completely with Theroux's understanding of education, that a boy who reads and learns just enough to mine ore, smelt and smithy a knife, sharpen and turn his blade to practical use will be the master over a boy who reads and lectures about all the same processes in the best universities in the world, just to be handed a penknife at his graduation. Which will be the one most likely to cut their hand?

While my understanding applies to many degrees that young men and women pursue in their late teens and 20's, I do not throw away the idea of university education. But a foundation of life created *only* on the books and essays and irregular lifestyle students enjoy in their formative years of adulthood, just because that's what everyone else is doing, without any tangible life experience to help them shape their path ahead, will be as fragile as the paper their textbooks are printed on.

To the teacher's dismay, I said goodbye to structured learning and embarked on a path of real-life skills and practical lessons through healthy, and sometimes unhealthy, trials and tribulations. I signed out of college for the last time, threw away my textbooks and carried home an empty rucksack which had been my ball and chain throughout my schooling. I applied to the Royal Air Force that same day while taking a slow walk home through the streets, fields and alleyways that I had grown familiar with while walking to or from school over the last six years. These same streets had also been my highway home at the end of the day, taking me back quickly to build dens, track animals and play in the fields behind my house. I can even credit my A grade in my English GCSE's to the roads that took me home, as a day before my English exam I realised that I had not yet read 'Of Mice and Men' and I was about to be tested for ninety minutes the next day! I found a copy under a dusty cupboard in the English department and managed to finish the novel during a very slow walk home. It would seem that the most important and nurturing part of my education was not the century-old syllabus, but the time spent walking to and from it.

Due to cuts in military funding and an incredibly difficult paper trail, it would take three years to start my military career. The following months saw me handing out hundreds of CVs and landing not a single full time job. The 2008 financial crisis was still making employment for young people very difficult, and with a recent influx of high school kids not wanting to go to college, it seemed all the jobs had been snapped up. I cut grass, worked as a waiter, had casual work at a plastic bag factory and gritted pavements with salt during the winter. In total I had become good at well over ten jobs between 2010 and early 2013, the most I earnt in a day was £100 for working sixteen hours through the night clearing snow. I drove a 1980's classic mini which my friends would pile into, and being young, wild, free (and skint) we would attend any opportunity to party that we had. I had a simple existence – stay fit for when I would start RAF training, earn enough money to keep my car on the road and enjoy time with my close friends. My parent's lives had both moved on, my dad choosing to live on a narrowboat and my mother settled in a rented house near where I grew up. Most importantly, both had started new love lives and stayed out of each other's way.

My mother had decided to move in with a very friendly, trusting man, introduced to me as Tom. I chose to live with my mother and Tom instead of my dad, a move people see unusual due to the unpredictable and sometimes explosive nature of my mother. I had decided staying with her would be the best course of action because I had casual work close to her new house, as well as friends and a girlfriend within a ten-minute drive. If I was to move in with my dad, I would have to start new work and friendships all over again, not to mention the narrowboat was very small for two grown men (in case you need further clarification, narrowboats are narrow in nature, and not ideal for persons over six foot like myself and my old man). I lived in relative harmony with my mother and Tom, accepting that the damage of the past was done, there was no need to live in a state constantly reminding myself of what had happened. Judging someone from a past act really wasn't on my agenda, I had no place for attitudes like that to influence my happiness.

Competitive swimming was a passion of my mother and father's, they were regional champions and had even competed nationally in their age categories, so swimming too became a desire she continued with Tom, in fact, it was at a competition that they met. They took their hobby and past time into new ventures and went into business as partners, teaching swimming lessons in the evenings, and during the day maintaining boats and small pleasure craft in a boatyard they had bought together. I soon ended up working for him doing odd jobs around the establishment for £20 per day. It was just a few weeks after starting work there when my active, healthy, forty-eight-year-old mother suffered a devastating injury.

My faith in discovering how the nature of all things is in a perfect balance was strong and I trusted that I could figure out what to do with any ill behaviour that came my way. But the seed of toxicity had been planted, and gradually my clear-minded appreciation of life started to overturn. Though my true nature had begun to emerge through the irregular education learned during the divorce of the two most treasured people in my life, the disruptive months where I had been exposed to and caught up in their awful conflict had caused a kind of rot to settle into my subconscious.

Like many other people before the recent growth of self-acceptance and openness towards mental health, I too saw depression as trivial and belonged to people branded as 'emo's' who needed a firm shake and a Happy Meal to cheer them up again. Until this time, depression was only a term I had seen in pamphlets and on TV programs. I was feeling an inability to healthily process the events that had transpired in the previous year, as if my very spirit had started to hemorrhage. While the sensations didn't appear to touch my emotions or attitudes, there certainly was an uneasy undercurrent that I would feel come in waves, lapping away in the background of my mind. The combination of the heartbreak from the collapse of my family, combined with the way I had my trust abused and events mentioned in the following paragraphs, acted as the ignition that led me to mental health troubles, self-harm and suicide – and I'm grateful for this every day. For through this adversity I found my calling… and a ferret named Bandit!

***

I was awoken at 0600 by the shaky, panicked voice of Tom.

"Charlie, somethings wrong with your mum."

The desperate tone in his voice was clear, so I rose quickly and followed him through the dark, windowless pea-green décor of the upstairs corridor to their bedroom. She lay in her nightwear, the duvet pulled away from her twisting, possessed body. She was a beautiful woman and always looked after her appearance. Her nails were very well kept and beautifully polished and shaped. Her hair, now moving jaggedly from side to side with her fitting head, would always be styled to perfection and never seemed to need a brush or amendment. Her minimal jewellery and delicate clothing complimented a stylish and consistently glamorous appearance she had mastery over. Her perfume was so subtle yet clear, and a dainty gold necklace with a small crucifix at the bottom hung from her neck – she always wore that dainty gold necklace.

All my senses pointed towards certainty that this should have been my healthy mother, but her body convulsed, writhed and shook like a flag caught in the wind. She thrashed violently from side to side, then would fall still and begin moaning, screaming and gasping for air. I vividly remember the bizarre way she would sit up between seizures though totally unconscious, push her hair back away from her face and straighten her attire, the same way she would do when getting out of the car, then collapse screaming and twisting again. I was competent in first aid to a qualified level and had on many occasions treated lesser medical emergencies in remote places while on small expeditions, but as most people who are first aid trained and have been exposed to medical situations will tell you, nothing prepares you for the real thing. Not only was this clearly a major medical episode, but the casualty was my mother and I didn't have a single clue how to help her.

I spoke to her and assured her she would be okay; we were looking after her. Interestingly enough the natural, compassionate action of talking to unconscious people makes perfect sense. In 1990, researcher R. Sisson proved in a large study conducted in the USA after years of speculation, that hearing is the last sense to leave a patient as they become unconscious. I made a phone call to the ambulance service and waited over an hour for the crew to arrive. By the time the ambulance made it to the house, Tom, my two sisters and I were around the bed of my now silent, unmoving mother. It would be a week until we learned that the illness that possessed her was a stroke caused by a tear in an artery inside her neck.

She remained unconscious for well past a week, and finally, when she gained consciousness, we came to the harsh realisation of the aftermath of such a tragic occurrence. Although she was now able to stay awake for short periods of time, she couldn't speak more than an illogical mumble, move more than a frown to indicate 'no', and a shallow nod for a 'yes' if she even understood what you asked her at all. The doctors doubted if she would walk again, but it was most harrowing to learn that she had totally forgotten all memory of who her family members were.

She would spend the next six months between Southend Hospital and a specialist ward of a hospital in London. While she was in Southend, a large town close to where I lived, I would endeavour to see her every day but only briefly to allow as many people as were there for her to spend time stimulating her brain, helping her to understand once more who the figures in her life were. The change between hospitals and the distance and time required to make such visits meant living and sometimes working with Tom

32

became incredibly strenuous, as we were both emotionally exhausted. Being constantly alongside one another in such an emotionally charged environment was also beginning to crack our once brilliant relationship. Tom spent more and more time away from work, and my responsibilities within their company outgrew my abilities as I had no experience in the fields of their business I found myself venturing into. At home, my time was now largely spent taking care of the house, cooking every night (as he had only ever made microwave meals for himself), cleaning and taking care of the domestic side of our lives. Tom continued to pay the bills and keep the business they had created alive, but from the first week she entered the hospital, my pay was stopped. I already received below the minimum wage so I could help them out as much as I could while their fledgling business grew, but even without pay, I decided to remain working for him out of a commitment to my mother's part in the company. Nine days after her stroke I had crashed my car, my only form of independence, while driving on the way to hospital one afternoon to see her. Without my own independent transport, hospital visiting hours and time with friends and family was dramatically reduced. Even if I did have a car, I now had no income for fuel or bus fares to be able to travel greater distances or at my own convenience. Their boatyard too was isolated from my hometown, so I would be brought to work by Tom in the morning but then had to rely on being given loose change for long bus journeys home, leaving me almost stranded from Monday to Saturday.

While living with an adult I thought I knew and could trust, Tom's true colours began to be revealed as his frustration grew day by day. Two months after her stroke, my beautiful mother still struggled to recognise her family and I could only see her once every week or so. As my situation became more troublesome, I started to drift away from my friends as most of the time they were inaccessible to me. Things went from bad to worse for my aspirations when my second attempt at getting into the RAF, my ticket out of chaos, had failed on an administrative issue. With my social and family life tearing apart, I too began to slowly unravel over the course of the coming months.

I began to notice my mental health had started to bubble up under my skin. From what started as a small wave, eroding its way through my mind from the saturation of all the turmoil of the state of affairs over the last few months of divorce, sudden illness and finding myself almost alone with my problems, an opportunity for the water to rise was taken, and the depression of that dark, cold ocean filled every harbour of my consciousness. It grabbed hold of any good thought and feeling in my life, ripped and slashed at it and filled the empty, bleeding hole with its own dark, twisted reverence. No longer was there a small amount of niggling erosion taking place at the subconscious of my usual happy self, now the cliffs of my mind had toppled into the abhorrent, frigid water below. To add to my inner taciturn was the poisonous environment I existed within. Just like my experiences during the divorce, I do not feel it's necessary to divulge many horrible stories at this peaceful time of life, but this one tame physical encounter illustrates the sometimes daily happenings I endured.

***

Tom, the man I had once looked up to, grabbed me around the throat and told me through gritted teeth, "you're still young enough for me to put you into care." I was seventeen and perhaps could have been 'put into' some kind of care provided for by the state, but the futility and irrationality of the comment raised some questions about Tom's legitimacy over his once so friendly character. To further illustrate the small-mindedness of the man, he told me how very upset and emotional he was. "That's my girlfriend in the hospital!" he yelled. I shoved his arm and pushed his hand off of me, stepped towards him and reminded him that "your girlfriend that you have known for a year has been my own mother for many more." The argument arose after I had decided to work for myself, traveling door to door in my neighborhood dragging a trolley behind me with a vacuum cleaner, bucket and sponge, cleaning cars for £5. After my first long, hard day of intuitive work that I had self-started from an old hoover in the shed, a tatty sponge I used for my own car, and some handily donated car cleaning detergent, I had earned £50. It was a small success by today's standards, but at the time I felt like a millionaire. It was the first pocket full of cash I had in weeks and I could clearly make a greater success of the simple idea. I could eventually contribute to the house and its upkeep and pay to repair my car, but until then I could now at least afford to get a bus to see my friends and my mother more frequently after work.

He was absolutely furious after our exchange, so Tom stormed out the front door and drove the short distance to my sister's house. When the door was opened by my beautiful little four-year-old niece, he pushed past her and yelled his frustrations with me at my sister, but immediately the hectic rant was shut down as no one knew me better than her.

She was almost ten years older than me and was the middle child between myself and our eldest sister, being one year her senior. My sisters and I would 'geek off' watching sappy films, playing our Saga Mega Drive, PlayStation 1 or getting involved with arts and crafts, making all kinds of strange things. Many blue sky days were spent with them in parks with their friends who were much older than me at the time but included me all the same. We still enjoy these kinds of calm activities rather than extroverted affairs; it seems the calm of visiting a country house or enjoying the solace of a walk through a park together is more fulfilling to our calm natures towards each other.

She knew the things he was saying about me were exaggerations or total lies (almost like she had read and applied the lessons in the previous chapter instantly, but without the soft and fluffy 'operate from a place of love' stuff I bang on about). These lies he was conjuring included me refusing to go to any form of work, even though I worked tirelessly for him for no pay and had begun earning money through my own endeavours. Realising his views of me weren't going to be welcome with either of my sisters, he spent the following days and evenings quietly spreading lies about me throughout my extended family who he was in constant contact with while my mother was in hospital, and greatly exaggerated how events unfolded to paint a picture of himself as a saint, and me a sinner.

It may be surprising for my readers, but I continued living with him out of what I perceive as a necessity, a kind of Stockholm Syndrome, or maybe just because it was the easiest option. I was a foot taller than him, much fitter and after seeing how much he struggled to lift and pull things in

36

the labour-intensive activities of the boatyard, it was clear I could have easily overpowered him in the times he became physical with me, but his psychological grasp deterred me from any confrontation. Perhaps I stayed living there because I felt he gave me no other option, or maybe my own determination not to break to his will kept me behind those closed doors, too proud to find help somewhere else. People who have experienced similar situations of domestic abuse as an adult, child or even if they had been a hostage to addiction may understand what I was experiencing mentally. 'Its better the devil you know' is a phrase that springs to mind. People prefer known hells to unknown heavens, and I surely did believe I wasn't capable or worthy of salvation or just a break from those times, no matter how many offers of help I received.

I was young and inexperienced, yet some part of me inside still felt compassion for him regardless of the ill-treatment directed towards me. I felt like the root cause of this pain we were both experiencing was due to an absence of love because of a deep hurt, caused by the suffering of the woman we both loved dearly. Regardless of the true colours a person shows after tragic events, if they are kept in check by love alone, then no one ever needs to know the capabilities of a bad person, as they would never truly understand their ability to do wrong with love supporting them all the while. Perhaps bad people only emerge not through their nature at birth, but as a reaction to love being withheld from them at any time of their life. Eventually, this reaction to the starvation of loving emotions becomes their miserable default for all circumstances. Though I felt for Tom and empathised with him, I never again did work for him, for I had seen how desperate and destructive the results of his actions were. Oh, and I never ended up living in childcare – I would like to have seen anyone try to put a seventeen-year-old me into care. I may have been young and dumb, but I had spirit!

***

Just the same way I had chosen to believe my mother's lies about my dad, I had chosen to believe this man's opinion and attitudes towards me over my own understanding of myself and I began to slip into destructive habits. The more I reacted negatively towards him and was lured in by his behaviour, the more I saw it reflected in the way I would treat and talk to others. Even to retaliate and escalate situations rather than taking a calm, collected approach was an unfamiliar thing to do.

I always approached conflict calmly and with maturity in mind, but the way in which I had allowed him to get beneath my skin, partly due to his persistent attacks and my mental state, I had sunk down to his level and became more of an easy target for him. I had totally ignored the wonderful truth about the connectivity and harmony in the unfolding universe I had stumbled upon at the church as a young teenager and lost the ability to notice the correlations in the world the way I had done before. My naturally loving decorum, fortified by testing events which had led me to a deeper understanding that there was a higher purpose to all things, had been totally abandoned. I chose to drown out the encouraging sound of my spirits contentment enjoying the world being exactly how it was meant to be and had shelved positivity. No longer could I see that my delayed initiation into the RAF, my struggle with relationships and my diminishing mental health

38

was a great lesson in learning the colourful peaks and troughs of life. I had a network of supportive adults in the form of grandparents, Air Training Corp staff and very close friends and some family, all of whom I had consciously chosen to ignore the love of and encouragement they gave me. I had failed to realise the essence of dealing with a challenging situation, that was understanding all things are just one thing, interconnected in a matrix we cannot begin to imagine or understand. Yes, a terrible illness had damaged the health of my mother, and of course, I was living with a sometimes violent, and often unfriendly man, but I had hundreds of things to be grateful for and a thousand reasons to wake up happy each morning.

The miracle of human conception should be enough for anyone to wake up, breathe in a fresh day and thank the incalculable circumstances that lead to the creation of you. Out of between 40,000,000 and 1,200,000,000 sperm, you are the one that beat the rest! You were once propelled into a twining of conscious passion experienced in a way almost unique to humans and entered a lottery of biology. The prize? A shot at making this unknown amount of time dressed up as a human being as joyful and inspiring as possible.

The world-renowned British astronomer, Fred Hoyle, so boldly stated that the likelihood of the random emergence of even the simplest cell is *less* likely than "a tornado sweeping through a junkyard and assembling a Boeing 747." Like the highest quality tailored suit, this pale blue dot we call Earth just so happens to be the perfect fit for life. The suit was purchased, the shoes were polished, and life has been swanking around in millions of different ways for 3.5 billion years. What about how perfect the position of our planet in the solar system is? How well balanced Earths chemistry is? What if our planet's water acidity was too high? What if we were too close to our life-giving star? What if hot, early Earth's carbon dioxide heavy atmosphere was weak, causing the liquid water below to evaporate into space?

And that's just taking into consideration this cosmically infinitesimal environment we have discovered ourselves in! These are a hand full of elementary scientific ideas to consider out of the truckload of possible outcomes for our precious planet and the emergence of life, all of which allow you to wake up in the morning with a choice to either shuffle groggily into your slippers and start thinking how hard life is, or embrace the miracle of every day and how unlikely it is you showed up to experience the perfection of life in the first place. Here's a wonderful extract from the beautifully wordy book by Bill Byrson, wordsmith extraordinaire of the book A Short History of Almost Everything (please check out his writing, they won't only make you look sophisticated while reading them, but they certainly will make you belly laugh too!) "To spell collagen, the name of a common type of protein, you need to arrange eight letters in the right order. But to *make* collagen, you need to arrange 1,055 amino acids in precisely the right sequence. But - and here's an obvious but crucial point - you don't make it. It makes itself, spontaneously, without direction, and this is where the unlikelihood's come in."

The miracle of life on Earth is incalculable and deserves strong consideration by all those who question what they have in their life to be grateful for. Life, this complex pattern of comings and goings, formless to form, flux and flow in a beautiful dance of biology which flourishes here on our blue-green planet is just another symptom of the universe ever thirsty to create new shapes and designs. We are, *you* are, as complex and fascinating as neutron stars, as convoluted a creation as the heavy elements, obscure like gravity and wonderfully bizarre like quantum physics.

The only difference between us and all other forms of the universe's complex patterns is that we have been given the gift of consciousness. We are the result of creations longing to experience and consider itself. For now, as far as we know, we are the only being witnessing the grand performance of nature, and tragically we forget that we too are all part of the act. We truly are the stuff of stars. One day, something new and entirely different will be made from part of the stuff of humans. So, enjoy cornetto ice cream while you can, one day in many, many years' time, part of your body may appear as the ingredients in an ice cream, or even part of a trusty old ice cream van that served it!

For now, in my own story of awakening that I'm trying to explain to you, the heavy, dark clothing of my depression fitted me perfect, and I wore it each day with gloomy pride (by the way, how am I doing? Well, if you've come this far I must be doing something right, or you're just a kind relative. Either way, thank you!) I had given up waking in the morning and being grateful for my existence. I continued to absorb more and more physical and mental battles from my once trusted guardian as his tales about what I had or hadn't done conned my family into disdain towards me, eventually rendering me homeless and without a minute of their help.

***

The summer of 2012 came and went, and the throngs of people buying into my car cleaning business ebbed away. I had earned enough money to repair my crashed car, sell it and purchase another classic mini, although this one was highly modified and built for track racing (the neighbourhood would never be quiet again). My mother had come home sometime before my eighteenth birthday. It was painful welcoming the shell of the once beautiful, proud businesswoman back to her home which for me was the battleground between Tom and I. What hurt the most was seeing her once youthful body slumped over in a wheelchair, barely able to recognise me or even string a sentence together. She would never know any of the events I experienced in the months while she recovered in hospital. The sickening feeling in my stomach at seeing Tom speak so softly to her is still sometimes overwhelming even as I write this, but I recognised the feeling of love in those moments between them and suspended my wavering ego to allow their love to prevail. She would raise her one good hand to touch his face while he held her. Her best attempt at I love you "iiiooo.. uuuve.. ooo" still lingers in my memory as she shared emotions with a man I had come to learn was far from how he displayed himself to the outside world and I could only hope she never saw any of his oppression. Sadly, as you will read, she did.

In the following days, we moved a mile down the road to a quieter area and a home where she could move around in much more easily. That winter, with great care and support, she had learned to stand and just about hobble around the house, defying all the doctors' predictions. When I was very young, she had told me that, "If you want something, you have to go and get it. Don't let anyone tell you what you can or you can't have." While this is a message told by parents and guardians every day all over the world, very rarely do they ever have opportunities to demonstrate this principle to their children. It was great to see that while her mind had been completely rewritten, her determination and unstoppable nature had remained intact enough to truly show the world her inner values. At her very core was a dedicated determination to only accept the things she wished to see come to light, so too is the way of so many great men and women who have walked this planet. No matter how small or frail, the quiet heroes of literature, science or prospectors for world peace emulate a strong, determined and heroic vibe to all their endeavours and accomplishments. It is their way and most honest nature. Not even a hammer and anvil could knock that out of them. My thoughts on such individuals best relate to Gandhi, Mother Theresa and Marie Curie. Do not let anyone tell you what you can or cannot have. It's a lesson that rides with me to this day and even while I write this book, I feel an overwhelming sense inside that I do not let the opinions of others become my reality.

Soon after she came home, I picked up my first full-time job working at a heavy plant maintenance yard earning £4 an hour. The work could be tough and dirty, but it was great working outdoors with my hands in the beautiful countryside location. I was always left to my own work with very little managerial input after I was recognised as being dedicated to my labour. It truly is fulfilling to always put your best efforts into any work endeavour.

I signed my own timesheet with a cheap black biro, but the value of that contract proclaiming the hours of my life I had traded for money was a serious consideration of mine. Some people feel giving minimum effort to work and clawing for maximum output as a better way to behave, but those hours spent earning your keep can never be bought back. If you work averagely or below, people will consider your seriousness to the commitment of giving away shavings of your life as a low priority of yours. If all effort is made to ensure that the signature you place on checklists, forms and paychecks carry with it the standard you set yourself to and the reliable nature of all work you have undertaken, the pathway for progression will surely be made for you. If you work diligently, you can only ever achieve the ability to stand back once your labour has been completed and proudly confess to yourself that this work, with your own hands and mind, has been completed to your high standard. Surely then, a good night's sleep and appreciation of the energy you bring to every endeavour you undertake will follow you all your life. This same attitude applies to relationships, artwork, book writing, sales calls, baking... the list is endless.

My dream to be in the RAF was still burning inside me and now my third application was being processed. My colleagues would laugh at my aspirations and promised me that I wouldn't make it. They would even go as far as to say that I would stay in the plant maintenance business for the rest of my life. It was here that I learned again another strange human trait. Just as Tom had fought me when I had earned money on my own initiative, my supervisor, a man we knew as Shorty, shot down my hopes and enthusiasm every time I mentioned my goals.

Shorty was very intelligent, funny and an incredible teacher – arguably the best employee of the business and I looked up to him greatly. However, he was miserable. I can only guess that his belittling of my aspirations was actually directed towards himself, perhaps to cushion the blow of failing to fulfill his aspirations as a young man to become something, *anything*, other than who he was. Perhaps his depression came from family trouble or simply feeling that life had been cruel to him, and he was too disheartened to get up, brush himself off and try again. I'll never know what bereaved my much-loved colleague so much, but I do understand that there was just no way a man with his mechanical skill and general intelligence winds up that despondent with the world and in a job as he had out of choice.

Regardless of how he had come to settle in the rut he had stuck himself in, nothing would give him more joy than speaking with me the day after one of my many RAF interviews, fitness tests or medicals. He relished in predicting what the medical officer would say and most jokes were aimed at my slim stature. I remember him saying "life is exciting when you're young and have dreams, but sooner or later life will wear you down", and "you'll realise how tough life is and you'll end up mediocre and fed up just like everyone else". I had to guard my ambition very closely and would often repeat in my many hours of solitude at the boatyard how exciting my life will be once I leave home, the place of such negativity and also escape this workplace and its belittling employees.

It's a startling estimate that for every negative comment you hear about a pursuit or belief of your own, it takes seven positive comments to reinforce your positivity about the subject in question. In a world where we can choose life as a friend or enemy, it can be hard to come to terms with the idea that positivity isn't hard-wired into our brains from birth.

John Cacioppo, Ph.D., studied the negative bias of our brains to discover that we react much more vividly to negative over positive stimuli. His research concludes that the reason for this was simple - it keeps us out of harm's way. Information about predators at the water's edge, a dangerous plant or hazardous area to walk over would have been crucial to our survival as early humans. On the other hand, positive information would rarely have served to keep us alive immediately.

Our brain's reaction to a challenging situation is stress and with it comes the release of cortisol, the hormone responsible for the sudden elevated heart rate, clammy hands and tense muscles. Stress is a biological reaction to an external encounter and acts as the body's caretaker that in times of danger provides the ability to move quickly. Both of these early evolutionary tools, our negative bias and stress, that once allowed humans to survive in the plains of Africa, now limit our potential to receive and react to positive stimuli in the twenty-first century where safety is a given, food is plentiful and our attention is fixed on thriving rather than surviving. Our collective mentality is pioneered by our best, most positive thinkers and aimed towards prosperity; though our natural individual tendency is to take in negative information and live accordingly from a negative source.

A similar occurrence with belittling taught me a lesson while back in that most infamous of ambition killing, mood sedating institutions,

46

secondary school. I vividly remember being told that in Physical Education I wouldn't achieve very highly as I wasn't a sporty student. In fact, my teacher had got it wrong, as I wasn't just not a sporty student, I wasn't a sporty human! My class had captains from the basketball, football, swimming and netball teams to name a few, and all competed in a regional or national level. The class students were made up of players from all our best sports teams… and me. I was the kid that was always picked last for a team! I can see why now, a noodle armed, lanky kid who was always reading and in the school's student council for five years wasn't the coolest guy in the playground when it came to ball sports.

The closest I came to a sports field was sitting in the sunshine to study for my geology exam (if that wasn't geeky enough, geology was a subject I volunteered to undertake as an extra grade!) I would be picked last out of the fifty or so boys and the team I would be placed into would give a disappointed sigh and tell me just to stay at the back, out of the way. I was told by a teacher that my physical skill was improving, but I had to learn the difference between the goal of my team and the goal the opposing team – no matter which way I kicked that ball it always went the opposite of my intended direction, followed by comments like "Are you stupid Charlie?!" No, I just hated sports!

Also, I was reminded to stop calling it a tennis bat, "it's called a racket," the teacher would say. Nevertheless, I refused to accept someone else's opinion of me becoming my reality. The overall grade relied heavily on a written exam and case studies, so I worked tirelessly at something I knew I could do well and focused on the theory of sport and writing practice essays. The teacher had stirred within me a passion to stand strong in my belief and I was set to prove him wrong about the D grade that, in his opinion, I was predicted to gain - the lowest grade of the class.

That summer when the exam results were given, a majority of the students expected to pass with A*s had come out with D's. My grade, however, was one of the highest in the class at a modest B, not an outstanding grade, but unquestionably an A* in the face of believing in your own ability. Not bad for the skinny boy who was always picked last!

I started to understand that no matter how well you do in life, your measure of success, how much you achieve or whatever you decide to dream, you're going to be talked down by almost everyone. You are going to meet with spiteful individuals and will be belittled by those who oppose your ideas, those who seek to sap positive energy from you and dominate you for the sake of their pleasure at seeing someone fail. Worst still, you will be miss understood or belittled by those that you love the most.

Seek to only come to everything you desire in life through a place of self-belief, a place where your opinion of yourself out-weighs the opinions of others. Abraham Maslow, famed psychologist who most notably suggested the theory of the hierarchy of needs, beautifully illustrated these points while explaining the top tier of the hierarchy, proclaiming a self-actualising person, or awakened, self-initiating person, is "independent of the good opinion of others." You, too, must be independent of other people's opinions of you. You must find a silence space within yourself to interpret what has been said, use it to fuel your drive and ambition, and move on from these people and their opinions with a sense of love and gratitude for the lessons you have gained from them, forging something precious to you from their attempts to derail your inner desire.

No amount of pressure from toxic people, especially at this point from Tom, could cause me to give up my pursuit of achieving the life long goal of getting into the RAF, showing them how reluctant I was to fail and how wrong their opinions of me were. While I had become very angry and had strayed from the positivity I had in previous hardships, the courage and determination I took from my critics bolstered a headstrong belief in myself. I made it clear that my ambitions and future success was going to be superior to their disbelief in me. This mindset wasn't an "I'll show you" attitude or a way to boast to others that "I told you so". I had my roots set firmly in the knowledge that any idea, dream or calling has come from within you, in the shape of a formless thought from an inner place of confidence and peace, and it came for a reason.

It always fascinates me how ideas and inventions can come from thin air. Once an idea or thought has been initiated in the brain, waves of thought can be measured and recorded, but prior to this decision to think a certain thought, where was the idea? An invention, for example, may start as a thought in an inventor's brain and evolve through the development process either on paper or in physical form, but where did the seed of thought originate from? It still surprises me that while I write, ideas and thoughts spring like colours from a painters brush on the canvas of the pages I am collating, bounding freely and easily from a formless, unknown place to take the shape of words and sentences to convey the deep thoughts, observations and contemplations of my being.

Marching to the beat of our own drummer, so long as it is for harmonious and peaceful outcomes, can only lead you on a journey to completion and fulfilment, or simply to show you a new path in your life. Regardless of its outcome, a thought has only come to you for a reason, no matter how trivial or silly it may seem. You have a right to the desires of your heart, and you should begin to believe that, while many fulfilling obligations and career moves may come your way, none make you feel more complete than that of a dream not necessarily come true, but a dream followed the full length of the path it wishes to take you. Fulfilment is a subjective topic, but the symptoms of wholeness, centredness and feelings of being aligned with a powerful, creative, loving energy is the same for all people. This very book is being written from that same place, I simply trust in the journey from an idea in my head (formless) all the way to physical completion (form). Regardless of how other people will receive my writing, it is perfect in both the experience of pursuing the idea and having the finished article in front of me for all to read who wish to do so. I see no distinction between a person wholeheartedly trying to achieve a small dream or ambition and a person who has completed ten of their life long goals.

Looking back to this time, there were many occasions that I collapsed in desperation about what I wanted to achieve or attract into my life. I've cried out loud at some points to life, God, the universe, Allah, or simply *the way* in all the harsh tests it gives to someone when they *really* want something, and I think it must have heard and decided to take me through a crash course on tough lessons until I learned the benefit within the suffering endured.

After struggling and fighting against setbacks and unfortunate relationships I felt I had been beaten up. I had first thought of life as a bully in the playground picking on me, shaking me down for my lunch money. But what I failed to notice was that life was not the bully and I was not the victim. Instead, all the roads that a character must take will be full of great struggles and disappointments, but only through them can noble victories be had, and incredible highs reached. It's simply a matter of perspective. Verse 36 of the Tao Te Ching perfectly illustrates this point clearly;

'That which shrinks
Must first expand.
That which fails
Must first be strong.
That which is cast down
Must first be raised.
Before receiving
There must be giving.'

If you have found yourself confronted with a bully or spiteful person, its right to say there must have been a time without the bully. After learning this concept, it's down to you to position yourself in life to hang out where the bullies aren't. If it can't be avoided and you're downtrodden by our metaphorical bullies, who in this chapter are not just represented as people but also as a culmination of many unfortunate events, remember that they will soon move along when you find the lesson in their motives and you'll be restored to inner peace once more. To expand on Lau Tzu's 36th verse with a touch of my own innate positivity, I would add;

'That which once was,
can be again.'

Be mindful that this addition to the extract from the 36th verse applies for both sorrowful experiences transforming into pleasant ones, and vice versa. The longer you hold back your truth and your true being, the longer you will live without true connectivity to your fulfilment and your personal legend.

Lessons from Spite and Kindness

'"Your eyes show the strength of your soul," answered the alchemist. That's true, the boy thought.' – The Alchemist, Paolo Coehlo

Sympathy

Meet your doubters with unconditional acceptance with who they are at this point in their lives. Do not compare them with the lessons that you have learned as no matter someone age or social standing, everyone is on a different journey and are all learning at a different rate. Accept their views and listen intently. Feel their words coming from within their unsettled person and readily give them love, regardless of their challenges to you or upset they cause. Family members often feel the need to settle disruptions amongst themselves, but sometimes you will encounter outsiders to your family who have found their way into your circle through relationships. They may seek to gain favour in your family over you, use you as leverage or jealously attack your energy as yours resonates higher than theirs. All acts of spite, retribution or debasement of credibility are an attack on someone's nature and purpose in this life. If you are struggling with a person who enjoys doing this to you, I ask you to read the fantastic poem titled 'Desiderata' by Max Ehrmann. Ehrmann's calming poem, written in 1927, can be applied to many areas in life, even touching into business management, but these words in particular really stand out for me when regarding the idea of listening to others regardless of what they are saying,

---

'As far as possible, without surrender, be on good terms with all persons. Speak your truth quietly and clearly; and listen to others, even to the dull and the ignorant; they too have their story.'

Ehrmann doesn't want you to listen only to those who you think have a good opinion of you, he wants you to listen to everyone. Everyone you encounter has a lesson to teach you, even 'the dull and the ignorant'. Their input will help you to follow your dreams through bolstering your resolve and confidence in your own opinions of yourself, so embrace their slander, cherish their doubtfulness and become an expert in converting negative energy with your own formula of positivity to help you succeed in all manner of areas that will bring your journey towards inner peace. What a person is really trying to say and express through their orations is always hidden behind their cruel behaviours. Why is he doing that to you? Why is she being so aggressive towards you regarding that position? Why did the client take his business to a competitor and review your company in an unreasonable way? Whatever the reason for the ordeals people place us into, the origin will likely lay with a belief they have learned from a young age. Maybe their view of the world was one of never having enough, or perhaps they saw that the nice guys don't do well in life just because their parent lost their job and as a result became bitter towards them as a child, then adopting that same attitude as an adult. Keep in mind your lessons in early life or perhaps adulthood and always strive to give love and sympathy, whether or not you receive it from them yourself. Contribute to countering bad with good and being a great example to those who wish to do harm by giving as much of your light as possible and feel that person with empathetic qualities. Whenever I embark on a charity challenge, tough journey across difficult terrain or set out to reach a lofty goal, I'm challenged by many people. I listen to their opinions and remind myself to really feel empathy from where their opinion is coming from, and to learn if what they are saying could help me. once I interpret their opinion, I simply file it away and any destructive or harshly opinionated comments enter into the 'Unwanted Opinion of Others' folder I have somewhere in my mind, taking from the comments only the lessons I need to embrace to drive me towards achievement. After I achieve a goal, I throw out these carefully filed ideas, safe in the knowledge I have disproved them. When you disprove your doubters, you will begin to form stronger resolve towards criticism and the process of self-belief will come easier and it will be much harder for negative comments to penetrate your new-found resolve in yourself. Remember this rhyme I've coined to help you in these times;

'You've said no, but tell me, how so?'

This maxim ensures that you have subconsciously considered what has been said and ensures you don't discount a comment, potentially missing the vital lessons it can teach you. Secondly, it addresses the idea of *you*, the title you use to address someone other than yourself. While doing this, you are acknowledging the fact that their experiences that have led them to form negative opinions of someone are the only experiences they know. It truly is their best thinking that has led them to sometimes hurtful conclusions and its right to feel sympathy for the fact they don't know a more harmonious way to interact with someone. The 'tell me' part of the maxim really allows you to search to find the information for yourself that is going to teach you a lesson worth understanding. 'Tell me' is an order, and while this maxim is to be thought of and not spoken, it allows a hypothetical situation where your imagination can probe and discover for itself the most valuable parts of their comments. Finally, the 'how so?' question is your time to passively challenge the opinion with your own confident and well-rounded opinion of your own abilities.

Everyone you encounter in your personal legend has a gift to give you, but its not always a pretty one, and it's very rarely wrapped up with a nice bow on top. Practice sympathy, practice feeling others emotions through their opinions, and love the 'dull and the ignorant.' My gift to you, if none of my words are ever remembered, is my trusty maxim, 'You've said no, but tell me, how so?'

Courage

It takes enormous strength to stand up for your beliefs when it seems the entire world is against you. Luckily, like footprints in the sand, success leaves its own clues and trail when we stop to witness the path someone has taken. All successful people in life, however you measure success or indeed however they measure their own, will leave clues behind for others to follow. These could be morning rituals, ways of thinking, schools they've attended, mentors or types of mentoring they've had and maybe even books they've read. While anyone can attend the same school as a multimillionaire, find the same mentor as a philanthropic business tycoon, or read the same books as a bearded wise man, there is one underpinning trait that I've yet to see learned by copying other people's routines or habits. This attribute can be harnessed in times of need or always be a part of their way of life. The trait I am alluding to is a person's ability to stand up, be counted, trust in their own strength of will and act accordingly. There seems to be no single word that accurately describes this mysterious ability witnessed during noble protests or in the heat of battle by countless men and women. Perhaps patients, bravery, nerve, boldness, tolerance, endurance all describe the characteristics of a person willing to stand up for their ideals, but for me, no word comes closer to best describing a persons inner strength like the word *courage*. Courage must be found if you are to follow your own path, for the world has a multitude of difficult people and circumstances you must face in pursuit of your goals. Courage can be studied as a principle for your approach towards your betterment of life through a particularly courageous hero of mine. I hope you will see for yourself how success through steadfast courage really does leave clues that perhaps you can follow. I do not believe that this world has events so greatly isolated from all others that a reflection of one cannot be found in the other. See these reflections for yourself in this man's story and endeavour to adopt the courage found deeply rooted in your own determination to be true to yourself, follow your path, and live your most worthy ideal.

It's 1916, the uniformed officers of the Arab Bureau in Cairo enjoy some downtime around a snooker table in the officer's mess. Their tailored uniforms are crisp and all the ironed creases are razor sharp. Toe caps of shoe's gleam as the sweltering Arabic sun fills all the windows and doorways which are so beautifully arched and decorated in an iconic islamic fashion. Each man, apart from genetic differences, is an exact replication of all the other uniformed men in the room. This was the age of British imperialism, and it's no-nonsense stiff upper lip was reflected in the pompous decorum of these men. A slim, blonde-haired, blue-eyed gentleman strides into the room with juvenile confidence, armed only with an absent-minded smile. His buffoonery had always set him aside from the other officers, and if it wasn't for his extraordinary education and intellect you would be forgiven for wondering why this man was ever commissioned as an officer by His Majesty, the King of England. To add to the obscurity of this gentleman, he was born illegitimate and as he grew into adulthood it became understood he may have been a homosexual – a criminal offence until 1967. How this misfit ended up a hero, hindering Turkish activity in Arabia, uniting tribes of the Bedouin and influencing the foreign policy of almost all western countries for the next 100 years seems unthinkable. I am, of course, referring to Thomas Edward Lawrence, better known to us as Lawrence of Arabia.

"I say, Lawrence", the officer's mess sectary exclaims as the maverick lieutenant ruins a game of snooker, "you are a clown!", to which Lawrence replies "We can't all be lion tamers". the quick and witty reply of Lawrence in the film epic 'Lawrence of Arabia' is a fabulous peek into the intelligent, testing, courageous and wholly self-actualising hero that was developed not in a single or handful of acts, but over years of courageously respecting his difference to other men. Defying the belief of his superiors,

Lawrence's repeated victories in the desert can only be attributed to his outstanding sense of self. The trust he gained of the Arabic people had never been experienced by an outsider before, and his willingness to embrace this privilege only developed a strong sense of self-esteem, the foundation of courage.

Lawrence is often seen wearing Bedouin clothing, including traditional headdress and a 'Janbiya' knife tucked into his belt. He is pictured with a revolver holstered on his waist band that was a trophy taken from a captured Turkish officer. Even his SMLE rifle was a gift from Emir Faisel, no less than the Arab king. No doubt, Lawrence was a fighting man and soldier and is widely regarded as being the first tactician in recent history to implement guerrilla warfare as the primary strategy of his forces, but Its not Lawrence's military might that has led me to attract your attention to him, but his unceasing desire to stand for something just, something bigger than himself and to believe in companionship. He had a deep longing for compassion, mysteriously writing a poem in the prelude of his masterful book 'The Seven Pillars of Wisdom' to an unknown entity only revealed to the reader as S.A. The poem's opening line is far too beautiful to leave out of this book which too is centred around compassion and love for humanity;

'I loved you, so I drew these tides of men into my hands, and wrote my will across the sky in stars.'

Lawrence writes freely and with passion when approaching matters of, as he calls, 'Man-and-man loves'. This extract from the Seven Pillars of

Wisdom beautifully summarises the intimate relationships desert fighters were involved in with their comrades;

'Friends quivering together in the yielding sand with intimate hot limbs in supreme embrace, found there hidden in the darkness a sensual co-efficient of the mental passion which was welding our souls and spirits in one flaming effort.'

Officially, Lawrence was opposed to homosexuality, but his unceasing desire to witness and document displays of affection between men made him special. Other officers were indifferent to the Arabs, but the position of trust and leadership that had been bestowed to this curious man led him to understand these people, not to judge them, but to honour their destiny by helping them free their lands from foreign invaders. While Lawrence's influence amongst the Arabic forces grew, it was painful for him knowing the British and French, once having rid the Arab peninsula of the problematic Turks, would divide the landmass between themselves as declared in the Sykes – Picot agreement of 1916 - and neglect to give the Arabs a share for their part in the bargain. Lawrence followed orders loyally, if not controversially, and fought hard with his Arabic friends for their freedom, knowing it would be taken from them once they had been used by the allied forces. After the war, with the bitter taste of betrayal inflicted to his friends in his mouth, Lawrence was invited to a private audience with King Edward V, where he was offered a knighthood for his exemplary efforts. Furious with the country's role in the betrayal, Lawrence declined the offer and stormed out of Buckingham Palace.

Lawrence's disagreement with imperialistic selfishness, status quo and steadfast belief in his own ability set him aside as a dignified subversive, needing no formal title or medal more than the credibility of his own name. He was later stripped of his rank and left the army, but secretly entered regular service as an airman in the newly formed Royal Air Force under the alias of John Ross. While stationed in Lincolnshire, he boarded for a while above a pie shop in the city of Lincoln, where he wrote his epic study of his war days with the Arabs. Unusually, Lawrence is also credited for the development of seaplane tenders, a kind of service boat that would assist seaplanes in all manner of shore-based tasks. His innate understanding of mechanics and problem solving was so that by the end of World War Two, some 13,000 servicemen's lives were saved by the Air Sea Rescue Service, a figure that could have been much lower if it wasn't for his hand in the development of the supporting vessels he co designed. Still driven by his pre-war years of academia, he wrote often, most notably he almost completed a book about his experience as a regular ranking airman in the RAF from the perspective of his former position at the rank of colonel. This book titled 'The Mint' was published posthumously as he died in a motorcycle accident, most likely orchestrated by security services according to some sources.

To put it simply, Lawrence's character, headstrong attitude and unyielding will to be his highest, most righteous self was the unorthodox foundation in which many military, academic and civil successes were built upon. Rarely is there a greater example of courage through self-belief as the achievements of Thomas Edward Lawrence. The British officer in command in the Middle East at the end of world war one, General Edmund Allenby, hits the nail on the head when he quoted "There is no other man I know who could have achieved what Lawrence did."

There are countless other heroes and heroines I admire and I draw from their courage daily. Set aside some time to research and discover the stories of such characters as Marie Curie, Shackleton and his crew, Sicilian hero Paolo Borsellino and Fred Rogers, who overcame great odds to change the face of American public television.

Surrender

The often scoffed at advice from parents and carers to young people regarding facing bullies is simply to walk away. How crazy we thought our parents were when the school bully gritted his teeth while spitting his or her best combo of curse words at us, or pushed, punched and pestered us into the most stressful of childhood ordeals - and their advice would be to walk away! This, however, is the exact approach that we should use when dealing with the wrongdoers in our life. When the sharp jolt of a spiteful comment catches us off guard, engaging into conflict with that individual or group of people will only serve to push the insult deeper. The ability to yield to the growing urge within yourself to intensify the conflict by reacting aggressively can be found when we simply surrender and sympathise with those that wish to harm us. Regardless of the trauma dealt, the ability to surrender to potentially painful occurrences can always be found within yourself, as peace can never be found by exacting revenge upon others. Taking the higher road is an impossible choice for a person who wishes to do us harm, but if we are to take their road, the lower road, they can meet us on their terms, in a place where they are much better suited and can remove any advantage to us. Learning to refuse to engage in a conflict will give you the courage to keep true to your own ability and ambition.

This is a personal account of a time I surrendered to a situation, took the higher road, avoided a fight and emerged the victor. It was boxing day 2018, 37,000ft above Europe with my other half, Chiara, on a flight to Italy. The flight was crammed with people returning home after spending Christmas day with their families or like us, flying to see relatives to celebrate the rest of the Christmas period together. The seats in economy class were very tightly packed. People were squeezing past one another in the aisle, bumping occupied seats unintentionally as they went.

I, too, had bumped the chair of the person in front of me by mistake as I took my seat, and even still it was a slight knock and not an event resembling a car crash. The hot-headed Italian man in the seat immediately turned around, angrily gestured to me and spoke loudly at me in his home language. I told him that I didn't understand what he was saying, and asked if he spoke English. He told me with a heavy Italian accent that the whole flight I had been moving too much and knocking his chair constantly while he was trying to sleep.

I was aware that I had knocked his chair that time as I sat down, but being a polite and frequent traveller, I always ensured I moved as little as possible to be as small an inconvenience to my fellow travellers. Instead of arguing and comparing my opinion that I am someone who is well mannered with his views of me being someone with little respect, I simply told him I was sorry, but what do you expect with such a long flight and very small seats? He cursed in Italian (while I don't speak that much Italian, I do know most of the swear words) and sat in silence the rest of the flight. As we landed in Catania, Sicily, he got up, went to the overhead locker to remove his bag, and to my surprise, leaned in towards me and offered me to a fight with the phrase "outside", with a firm gesture to the rear of the aircraft.

He stormed out of the cabin, and I diligently proceeded to follow, refusing to be disrespected and misunderstood by a man who only knew me by the position of my seat in the aircraft. To my surprise, he wasn't at the foot of the stairs below the aeroplane, but I could see that he had already proceeded to advance towards the front of the passport control queue. Perhaps when he mentioned "outside", he meant outside of the airport, as if our fight was in the same category as lighting a cigarette. Just imagine, "Please refrain from lighting cigarettes or beating up fellow passengers until you have exited the terminal building."

I rushed up to his position in the queue, tapped him on the shoulder and told him "we are outside now, is there something you wanted to say?" Now on the back foot, the man looked startled and afraid to engage in escalating his aggression any further. Again, I pressed him if anything was wrong, to which he told me there was nothing and I should leave him alone and not to touch him. I held out my hand of which he shook, I looked him in the eye and said "bene", or in English "good."

My surrender from the situation during the flight and my silent withdrawal gave me the courage to really assess the situation and call the man's bluff. I did not wish to escalate this encounter until it became physical and so I simply surrendered the idea of a fight between us, yet I did seek to defend my honour and establish to the man that, while his way was that of conflict, mine was that of harmony will all persons, be them chair kick accusers, playground bullies or nasty employers.

Some unfortunate situations do call for physical interventions as I will discuss in later chapters, but unlike running away or cowering from the sometimes serious losses in your life, be it emotional or physical, surrendering to the quiet place within is very different from cowardice.

When we surrender to the all accepting and loving place within ourselves, we are giving our problems to the mind of god, the creator, or more simply put, allowing *the way* by getting out the way. Our highest sense of self is in subtleness and gentleness, for only there can the waters be calm enough to see through, winds settled enough to build, and temperatures mild enough to thrive. Dealing with emotional and physical stresses while in an agitated mind will only leave you confused as to why such seemingly horrible things happen to you, and how you should appropriately react to them. Surrender your judgment of the situation. Surrender unhappy feelings towards others. Surrender thoughts about where the lessons are in our darkest times and know that equilibrium is on its way. Let go of what you wish to go from your life. Draw backwards and surrender, and you'll advance towards peace.

Judgment and Intuition

"If prayer is you talking to god, then intuition is god talking to you." –
Wayne Dyer

I had begun to learn to overcome or embrace the lessons from certain situations that had formerly caused me to lash out angrily. Instead of angry action, I now opted to listen to the quiet voice inside that is always much stronger in its own belief and energy than the belittling and doubtful opinions of those who will choose to upset you. However, slipping silently under the radar of my seemingly strong will power and overall persona was a mental health cataclysm, bubbling and boiling away at the core of my person.

I was awoken early on a weekend morning by Tom. I registered a problem due to the unusual time and tone in his voice when I heard his muffled speech from his and my mother's room next door. He knocked gently on the white plywood door of my bedroom and asked to speak to me. I rubbed my eyes and quickly removed the blanket of slumber allowing me to clearly see his solemn face in the half-light of the morning coming through the blind. He proceeded to tell me that due to how hard it was looking after my mother, he was leaving.

Since she had come home things had been very tough. Dressing, feeding and bathing her was a challenge that Tom and I both shared out of our love for her, though we still barely tolerated each other since our falling out months beforehand. He told me that not only was he leaving because of his struggle looking after her and running the company they had formed, but also because our unfriendly relationship together was affecting the situation between him and her. She would wish we would just get along, though she hadn't seen and couldn't understand that he had been physically abusive and aggressive towards not just me but also other individuals in the time she had been in hospital. I didn't tell her everything that had happened between Tom and I as she didn't have any reason to believe he was an aggressive person at all and she wasn't in the right mental or emotional state to receive such news about the man she loved. I told Tom he was under no pressure to stay; her care didn't have to be his responsibility and I wouldn't judge him if he did leave. In fact, I admired his determination to help my mother's life return to some kind of normality, though he couldn't continue down the same road to recovery with her. We shook hands, and he left the house with a small bag of his belongings.

Concerned with the turn of events, my sisters and I wondered what had really happened to make him leave so suddenly. He had a lot of opportunities to leave before renting and moving to a new house and continuing to grow their business, and in this time my mother had formed a strong dependency on him. Something just wasn't sitting right with the whole event and though I had no judgments about his leaving, my intuition was screaming an alarm to me. My sisters too couldn't help but feel an intuitive feeling that he wasn't telling us the whole truth. Soon after he left, my mother grew quiet and unwilling to share any of her opinions or even convey any feeling of good or bad towards his leaving.

A few days later after a handful of phone calls between the two, Tom quietly and mysteriously moved back in. His nature ever since she had been in the hospital was to be very covert, unwilling to share with me where he was, or when I would see him again. This past sneaky history didn't alarm me at the time, but now I felt like somewhere within me, I knew something wasn't right.

He had eventually come back after she had begged him, telling him that mine and his relationship wasn't a big issue. I was soon to be leaving for military service anyway and would be out of the house, away from him. That was the point I realised how extreme her dependency on him was and how she had started to outgrow her love for her own son, daughters and her self-respect. This once strong, independent businesswoman had totally handed over control of her life to a man she had only known a short time, a painful thing to witness knowing how cruel he could be. This was an important benchmark in the relationships between us and my home life. I could now clearly understand that her willingness to regain her own independence and emotional strength had been completely bypassed. In exchange, all control, responsibility and respect for her family had been transferred to his hands. She had given Tom the means to leverage his favourable, dependency-based relationship with her over me.

Tom quickly dominated the household. All finances were now in total control of him. He would decide how much money my mother would get to herself from council allowances and company profits. He controlled her bank card and account and would always find an issue when she would allocate time to spend money to buy a coffee at her favourite shop in the high street or if she tried to purchase anything online. All comings and goings of the home were strictly monitored, and though Tom had previously shaken my hand and drew a line under the fact that we didn't get along, he again spread more and more lies about me through the family. It was easier to buy into his story than the words of a so-called troublesome kid.

In the whole time this story lapses I received no more than two or three phone calls from relatives. On the odd occasion that I saw them in the flesh, I was always advised that perhaps I should be easier on my mother and help Tom out more around the house. I never received a phone call or visit to the house to converse with me and gain understanding as to whether what they had heard about me was true or not. I didn't seek any affection or pity for the situation I was in. Indeed, I never asked for it, but I believed it was my burden to put on a brave face, and trust that the truth would be exposed through my passive protests and tolerant temperance against his antagonising behaviour. Finding his story cheap, every person Tom had aligned to his agender bought every tale he told. They had created their own reality of me, and I never had an opportunity to protest my innocence. Never has the saying 'the only thing worse than not knowing the truth is only knowing half the truth' been so appropriate. Tom never directly approached me when he had a problem with something concerning any action of mine, instead, he would spill his disdain over the now completely corrupted mind of my mother, who he would then use as a puppet to manipulate my feelings.

To summarise how downhill my situation was becoming, I was now completely cut off from any support in my so-called home, my family had become indifferent to me and now even my sisters, believing the words from our mother first planted by Tom, started to doubt my innocence. Even though we had made up, the relationship with my father was troubling me as I wrestled with the grief from guilt that followed from my actions as an angry young man during their divorce. Although he had told me I never lost his compassion, I felt I didn't deserve the love he offered unto me.

The despair of the situation I had landed myself in had become my only companion of the ocean of depression I was a host to. The twisted, weakened structure of my mind, heart and spirit splintered as the weight from the failing love and support of my family bore down on me. The fire from the poisonous divorce I had been used as a tool in had left a rotten hole wide enough for Tom to fill with his own toxic agenda. The heartache of seeing my mother suffer immeasurably was only made worse when I began to realise she was turning her back on me now too, in favour of the man who laid hands on her son. The only male figure in my life, my dad, who I loved dearly, I felt I could not share my problems and situation with wholeheartedly.

Confusion was my daily struggle, as I hadn't yet had time to recognise that a sickness of the mind was devouring me. Again, I could have left, there were places I could go, but during that time I still needed to remain settled and hold out for my RAF start date – moving away from Essex would have been a step backwards. further adding to the feelings of depression was doubt. I doubted myself and started to wonder whether the

70

things being whispered about me were true. I wondered that perhaps I was as bad as I was being made out to be. When your own mother decides to believe lies about you it's hard to trust yourself and your own intuition regarding what you know or *think* is right. Maybe you, the reader, will understand that feeling, though I hope you never have. I was aware of how animals, both domestic and wild, are nurtured, raised and supported by a matriarch, a mother and provider of limitless love. It pained me deeply to see my own mother withdraw her open affection for me and divert the loving energy towards Tom. I didn't feel jealous, but I certainly felt betrayed. With pressure mounting, the noose I placed around my neck through my pride and unwillingness to seek help began to tighten.

Christmas time, 2013, would become etched in my mind as one of the most important dates in this dark period. Tom had been treating me surprisingly kindly for a few consistant days. He noticed my socks had holes in them, so he bought me a new pair – a small gesture of kindness, but it was very unusual for him to be kind to me. He ordered a Chinese takeaway meal for us all to enjoy together, again another out of character thing for him to do. My intuition screamed at me again as I sensed some strange manipulation was taking place.

The next morning, I was totally baffled to discover that Tom had left home for the second time. He hadn't come and seen me to explain his leaving as he had done before, so I asked my mother what had happened. In her best muffled, stammering English, she informed me he had left because he couldn't stand me any longer. A fair reason to leave if that is how he genuinely felt, but why would he treat me so kindly the previous day if I couldn't be tolerated? Again, Tom's motivation to leave didn't feel right, and my old friend intuition had finally pieced together a theory after months of strange behaviour, and I felt I finally had an answer, though it was one I didn't want to believe. I knew it was totally plausible that Tom was enjoying passions with another woman while my mother was in the hospital or while she was housebound and unable to move freely. Alone, he had been carrying on the swimming classes and competition events, often staying away late into the night all around East Anglia. She had tried to swim again but she could barely walk, let alone front crawl. She would often obsess over how everyone would feel sorry for her and become judgemental due to her condition. She was a very proud person, but unfortunately sometimes too proud. Tom would go out most weekends without her, and many nights during the week too. I had no suspicions at first that he may be giving his affection to another woman, but after his unusual behaviour in the last week, the sudden disappearance and the subsequent blame being shifted away from her to me, I suspected foul play.

One thing was for certain, Tom had been weaving lies about me in an effort to gain favour and leave me in the dark, and now with that complete, a perfect prelude to blaming me as the reason for their breakup had been set. He couldn't tell people he was leaving because it was too hard looking after a disabled woman out of duty or guilt, nor could he tell them that he'd been running off with another woman while she struggled to move around the house and look after herself. The easiest way out was to blame the rebellious, teenage son, who had been painted as an indifferent, immature asshole to Tom and his mother. This, of course, was the bare bones of the lies all people involved had come to believe.

The truth is that during this time I was working as many hours as I could for my employer, and I had started my own online collectables shop on the side. My weekends were spent volunteering to help train a new generation of young leaders at my local Air Training Corps squadron and I worked tirelessly on my military aspirations by practicing exam questions, studying and exercising sometimes twice a day for many hours. Again, I don't feel it's necessary to retell all the physical and mental abuses my mother and I were enduring, but I remember a close friend telling me my life was like the soap opera EastEnders (to my American readers, think of the SitCom friends, but add alcohol abuse, depressing storylines and of course a good ol' English Pub). There was just no conceivable way in my mind that I could be to blame. I was far from perfect, but there was no way I could have been held accountable for him leaving so suddenly without warning. That evening I realised the reality of a lie believed.

***

My sister came over to the house sometime around early evening. She had been talking to Tom and had been told that he had left because of me (what 'because of me' means I never would fully discover). I can intensely recall how my mother sat on the staircase as my sister confronted me, demanding that I had to change. She told me how I was being irresponsible for not caring for her well enough and how it was my behaviour that caused him to leave home and our mother behind. She needed Tom and couldn't function without him, it was my duty to march to the beat of his drum, do as he said and restore our relationship to the way it was prior to the stroke. Little did she understand the state of control we had been living in under his manipulative, dominating rule and how I tolerated the abuse so I could focus fully on reaching the starting line of my career in the military. She never had experienced how damaging caring for a severely disabled parent could be. She did sometimes visit to help, but I had lived caring for her from morning to night, night and day. The confrontation became more heated when I decided I wouldn't take being spoken to like that by someone who really should know me better, someone who should have thought to question Tom's story first before simply believing it. The back and forth of the argument came to an end when, for the first time, I aired my concerns about the likely hood that Tom had interests outside of the house with another woman. Immediately, I was stopped mid-sentence and told how wonderful he was for looking after her and how I should respect him. The obscenity of the retort from her defied my understanding. How could someone so close to me believe the words of an outsider to our family, who she knew herself could be manipulative, over mine? The power of a lie was truly impressive. Throughout the entirety of the argument, my mother sat in silence, wanting neither to calm the situation or add to it. Knowing she wasn't going to volunteer information regarding the facts about where Tom spent his time or how poorly he could treat her and I, I still foolishly tried to get her to comment on aspects of the argument, yet she wouldn't account for the things I knew she had experienced.

Noticing there was no hope for my views to even be considered, I disengaged from the fray and rushed past my mother to my bedroom. I grabbed my rucksack, filled it with some spare clothes and said my goodbyes. I didn't expect my mother to understand any of what was happening. Before I left the front door, my sister delivered one final comment that was not one of her own, but in fact an ultimatum from Tom that he had asked be delivered to me, 'leave home and I'll come back to look after your mother. Do not return'. I was leaving in a couple of months' time for military service and couldn't look after her when I was gone. Every family member involved in the events of the time had abandoned me and decided to believe Tom's narration of events. I was between a rock and a hard place, while the whole time all I truly cared for was that my mother would be happy, healthy and safe. I was left with only one option after hearing my ultimatum (which seemed more like a ransom note) and that was to realise my defeat had been total, accept the demands made against me and leave home behind. I had to trust that perhaps this would be the best option for her health and happiness. Through all the violence, lies and betrayal that we had endured, I ended up homeless and the accomplished black sheep of the family.

I tossed my bag onto my shoulder, turned away from my home and headed a mile down the road to the nearest woodland. The air was cold and the farmers' fields bordering the great woods shone in a weak orange glow of the lazy December sunset, complimenting the wild, burning colours of the leaves that had fallen at the foot of the trees. Some leaves were still drifting downwards as they separated from their branches and were highlighted in golden auras as they glided through the air around me. From the tree tops came the occasional craw of a solitary crow, bracing the cold and joining in the evening chorus of different songs as the birds sang farewell to the departing daylight. The ground underneath me was cold and sturdy, my pace slowed as the troubles in that house and months under its roof grew further and further away. Every step I was now taking took me from the complications in my life not just at that time, but from the last three years. In the instant that I was forced to leave that toxic environment, I regained total control of my outlook on myself and the situations around me.

The hand that I had been left to play wasn't a good one, but if I played my cards right, I would get out of this as a much greater person. On my back was a small collection of belongings in a rucksack and in my head was the dream of the moment the military would take me away from the only life I had known. With just a few precious items including a sleeping bag, warm clothes and change of underwear, I found security and independence quickly approaching, though I didn't even have a place to spend the following winter nights other than between the ancient trees of Hockley woods. Henry the 8th used this once great forest as a royal hunting ground five-hundred years ago. The prehistoric woods, once enormous and wild, were now a little less than a couple of miles wide and well managed. It was once fit for a king, but now it's soul occupant would be my vagabond self. The cold shadow of the trees I had now reached reminded me that we can always step back when it gets too hot, just like we are free to step out into the sun again if we get too cold. Memories from my time by the church flooded back. Everything was working out exactly as intended, whether I could see it as a good thing or not. This was a lesson that had bought me through an awful divorce, but through the tumult of time, I had forgotten the pacifying message. Again, I was reminded of how every moment is in perfect collaboration with another if you just approach each situation with an open mind. I could see clearly how my innocence could be proven by Tom's demands that I leave, because if I truly was the reason he walked out on her, he would come back straight away now that I had left. Willing to

76

place my bets on the fact of his leaving was nothing to do with me, I guessed that he wouldn't return even after he discovered I had abided by his order to leave. He had underestimated me greatly and wrongly predicted that I would stubbornly defy his blackmail and remain at home so he could demonstrate to his followers that I was indeed as bad as he had made me out to be.

These cold woods were now my warmest companions and I felt I couldn't turn to anyone human as my sense of pride was at stake. Though I had voluntarily made myself homeless (I could have ignored his blackmail after all and stayed at home), I felt that I should use that same bold confidence to find my way alone and unaided as far as I could. Perhaps pride kept my head held high and I refused to ask for help, I didn't tell of my homelessness to any of the few supporters I had. I knew I couldn't ask many of my immediate family for a place to stay because they had fallen for Tom's lies and I wouldn't be welcome. Though I was confident in my character and quick adaptations to change, I felt shameful for not being able to provide a flat or bedroom for myself and frustration at not being self-sufficient enough to even begin to look after my own issues. I was even more frustrated that I had allowed Tom to get the better of me. I still had work, but only drew a tiny income, just £300 per month – rooms in Essex were at least £400 in rent alone and even then, it would take a while to find a place and move in. But I did have clothes, a few folded notes of money in my pocket for food and most importantly a whole lot of courage. I don't remember how many nights I slept without a roof over my head, but when faced with the crippling uncertainty of homelessness, time seems unimportant. You live moment by moment, not in a free-spirited way, but essentially in survival mode.

This is when the lady that was to become my 'adopted mum' pulled me from the wreckage that entrapped me. Never will a day pass where I will ever be able to repay the love and hospitality she gave to me, not even if I lived a thousand lives. Samantha was the mum of my best friend that I grew up with through secondary school. They knew how challenging my world had become, but I didn't allow the full extent of the details to reach them in the months leading towards that day fearing that I would worry them to death and cause them to seek pity on me. My ego was strong, and I considered taking the charity of others as a weakness.

My palms were sweaty as I stood on the doorstep of Samantha's beautiful home in a sleepy village street in Hockley, clutching a black rubbish sack of bundled belongings tightly in my hand. That afternoon before I arrived at their front door, I had snuck back into my mother's house (I still had a key) and quickly packed a few more things into a rubbish sack. It was late at night and in only a weeks' time, it would be Christmas. The neon glow of the Christmas lights adorning their house alternated between bright green, blue and red, and shone brightly on the shiny plastic surface of the stretched black bag. My head was warmed by the hood of my jumper, but the cold made my neck long for a scarf. I reached forward, leaning over the brilliant white of the light-up snowman hugging the wall in festive cheer, and pressed the small white buzzer mounted next to the door in the red brickwork. The doorbell chimed the tune 'Westminster's Quarters', the same song played by Big Ben in London. I peered into the dark of their

78

house through the glass door, my gaze looking past the coats and shoes hanging in the hallway which were competing for space with the amount of Christmas decorations set in random perfection. A warm glow of light filled the corridor as I saw the living room door open and ignite further the colourful and detailed décor of their house. Samantha curiously flicked on the hallway light and looked towards the door with a frown, wondering who on earth would be ringing their doorbell this time of night. Noticing my figure, she joyously opened the door and welcomed me inside, and I left the cold there on the doorstep.

Out of the hundreds of times I visited that house, never did I see Samantha unhappy upon answering the door. She was the embodiment of love and if her smile didn't warm you, then her embrace surely would have. Never have I met such an honest, warm and loving person in all my life. She truly was one of god's most complete works of goodness. Theirs was a simple, calming, homely kind of house, festooned with picture frames, books, ornaments and keepsakes. The living room was simple and comfy, with each seating position being 'owned' by each family member, you would always find them in the same seats all the years I had known them. Extensions over the years had made the layout of the house irregular, but totally practical for their needs. Samantha's favourite animals were dolphins and birds, both great symbols of peace and freedom. Johnathon Livingston Seagull was her favourite read, and she always yearned in her heart to wander freely like Johnathon and explore far enough to 'touch the face of God.' But it was always the very English red breasted robin that she most adored, and she famously covered every spare corner of their house with pictures and small statues of the beautiful little bird. This time of year, tinsel wound its way around the staircase, table, TV cabinet and just about everywhere else for that matter. Not even the dog was spared, and if it wasn't for the cat being so temperamental, she would have been covered too! In the same way that the woods have their own seasons they look best dressed in, so too did this house have a different feel to it as the year went on. In spring, traditional seasonal food and Christian celebrations found centre stage. Summertime would see all windows open, allowing tendrils of sweet, warm air to explore and divide itself amongst the rooms, while the garden shed was host to many water fights or boyish tomfoolery. Autumn bought orange and red leaves in enormous piles in the garden and the placing of summer jackets into wardrobes in exchange for large cold weather coats, all to be hung in their place for the next six months beside the front door. But, just as the bluebells and snowdrops flawlessly suit the juvenile birch tree thickets, wintertime and Christmas was the season longed for by the house's interior and by Samantha herself. It wasn't a massive house, but that didn't matter – It was perfect for them, and they were perfect for me.

She was outraged at what I had told her had happened between Tom, my mother and I over the last few months. Like many other people who had offered to help me find my feet after her tragic disability, I had turned her offers to help me down. Samantha was a lady of small stature, but enormous courage and fight. She too had experienced a difficult upbringing with her parents and sympathised with my circumstances, so she reminded me of her offer to live there while I awaited my RAF start date. I can just see now how her mood turned from quiet sympathetic comforts to blood boiling rage as she ranted about how she would "knock sense into that Tom". I had seen her angry, stern persona a handful of times, and I was always glad to have such a ferocious person supporting me. I still believe she could have stopped Julius Ceasers advance on ancient Britain single handedly if she was alive two-thousand years ago! With nowhere else to turn, nights drawing colder and abundant comfort and love being freely given at that house, I accepted their offer and, like a stray brought in from the snow, their home became mine too.

I emptied my rucksack, set down the few belongings beside the sofa, and entered into my first deep, peaceful sleep in months. Little did I know, I would call that sofa home for the next three years. The first week living there in that perfect home was a time of real reflection. I had hardly any money, all of it had been used fixing my car (It was undrivable due to a minor breakdown prior to leaving home), getting the bus to my low paying job and buying train tickets to the RAF appointments across the UK. I had almost no way of contributing to my new household where I slept in the living room, while almost all my junk was stored in their garage. My mother hadn't been in contact with me, my extended family knew about my leaving, but hadn't checked to see where or how I was living, and only one of my sisters knew where I was sleeping. The shock of finding myself on the cold side of my mother's affection, homeless, sleeping in my car (on one very rainy occasion) or in a sleeping bag in my favourite woodland, had compounded the depression that was so deep-seated into a comfortable pain. I would wrap the depression around me, and within the pain, I found a kind of comfortable solitude. I had, however, just passed my final selection test and had a confirmed start date at the recruit training school, RAF Halton. I clung to that date in sheer desperation. It was my golden ticket. Not only would it catapult me into a military career and childhood dream, but it would act as a ladder I could climb to escape a troublesome life. I also believed I could now simply seal up the depressive madness eating away my insides and pretend nothing had happened. So that is exactly what I did.

With Christmas upon us in Samantha's house, I was once again part of something I had lost four years ago with the separation of my parents - a stable family. As Samantha's relatives and friends came around for gift giving and food eating throughout the Christmas period, I was adopted not just by her, but by her entire network. The love I received from their neighbours and cousins alike was unlike any experience I had had before. Here I was, a recent vagabond edition to their family, barely holding a job, a broken (but very cool) classic mini and no real accomplishments, yet I was being given love by near strangers in such a beautiful way it that truly lifted my spirits and gave me hope once again. The thoughts of dark, deep waters that would consume my mental wellbeing were illuminated by the graces of love, and I humbly shelved all thoughts of depression. I let my past lie, unwilling and unable to delve into the ground and treat the illness by the root, as if the sun shining on a weed would kill it. While their love was incredible, without all the right guidance and professional help to treat myself healthfully, I boxed up my issues and stored them away deep within my consciousness. Alas, it would be this kind of action that would eventually cause me to choose to end my life.

***

After Christmas, I called my mother to check up on her and find out where Tom was. Just as I had expected, Tom hadn't moved back in following my leaving. He hadn't even seen her since the day he left! His promise to return if I withdrew from their lives had now been proved, through my courage to accept homelessness, to be a bluff. He had used the whole dramatic blame game and spiteful ultimatum to make it seem like I was the cause and instigator of make-belief events in that unsettled household. Though he didn't expect me to leave, after putting that incredible emotional pressure on me, he left me with no other choice. I was never going to let Tom think he could play me like he wanted to and smear my name, even if it meant becoming homeless in the process. I was baffled by the knowledge that he hadn't returned. At the time, I believed that his action, or non-action, would have been enough evidence itself to prove my innocence, but I was still considered an outcast and trouble maker by my family, even with the knowledge that he hadn't returned to look after my mother like he promised.

Though I felt awful that she must have come to the realisation that her partner, and to some degree her carer, wasn't the man she thought he was, a tremendous weight had been lifted off my shoulders. Those who blamed me for these difficult situations had no other alternative than to question Tom's motivations or turn away from the blinding truth of the situation and intrench themselves in their stubborn opinions. I'll let you imagine the names I called him after the phone call I had with my mother about his non returning, but here's a hint, one of them rhymes with 'anchor'. While the unfolding truth enabled my sisters, who formerly supported Tom, to see the honesty in my words and actions, they were shocked at my bold move at temporarily living homelessly, and deeply hurt that Tom would use my mother as emotional blackmail to shame me.

I'd like to introduce you to the psychological phenomena known as the 'Entrenchment Effect' or 'Backfire Effect', you may have experienced this yourself. When given overwhelming evidence proving a belief of yours to be false, you may have retaliated with "but that's not what I read in the…" or "but that's not what my father/mother/sister/brother told me.." or even better "I'm sure that was right, I saw it on Facebook!" When one is faced with irrefutable evidence on the contrary to what they believe, they rehearse to themselves why they believe it, further entrenching their certainty. Drawing on this phenomena, most of my relatives refused to acknowledge the unjustified actions bought against me and more importantly my mother, and they subsequently slipped further and further away from believing in the true events we had experienced. I did not wish to push my story onto anyone, figuring that true, loving family will ask questions and discover the truth in their own time.

Before I left Essex and with Tom now out of the home, I had a precious few weeks to spend caring for my mother when she needed it and seeing my childhood pets, Socks the cat and our wonderful dog Dusty. We had patched up our relationship enough so that I was able to stay the night a few times before leaving, and I tried to get over to her house as often as I could before I left. January was a time for quiet reflection both over Christmas with my new adopted family, and occasionally with my Mum. The last few years had been rough, but I'd come out wiser and bolder. With RAF employment now a certainty, I was approaching a settled end to a

84

dramatic period of my personal life. Tom still wasn't living there but did come to pick my mother up to go out on dates. I would wait patiently with a friendly demeanour by the door every time he came, it was important for me to let her see that I wasn't the hostile man I had been made out to be. Having learned many lessons along the way, I was ready to approach tough people with love and forgiveness regardless of all wrongs they had committed. Tom wouldn't be an exception. I didn't expect him to shake my hand or even be happy to see me, but a polite, loving gesture towards harmony is sometimes all it takes to help people realise you truly identify with peace and carry no resentment within you. I decided I would settle for a polite nod between us if I ever had an opportunity to make eye contact with him.

Every time I waited, he would pull up in his car, always looking forward in a trance-like fixation, unable to bring himself to look at me. My mother would hobble to the car, dragging her bad leg behind her. I would help when necessary, but being the proud woman she was, she didn't enjoy anyone helping her, though I would sometimes do so anyway. Tom, however, knowing I was waiting for him so I could give him a friendly hello, never once left the car to so much as open the door for her while I was in his or her vicinity. I, the victim of a witch hunt led by this man, was mature enough to see the pointlessness between our hostilities. Our conflict was affecting my mother greatly, but he still refused to meet me on the higher road, settling for the comfort he had found in the lower one. I remember her desperate pleas for us to get along, I told her I would do what I can to bring around harmony, but ultimately it was down to him to also decide to come back to her home. Even if he didn't acknowledge me, I would happily stay out of his way in order for him to return and pursue life with her once again. I was already living in a different house with a different family most of the time, but it was clear he had too much pride to return to her before I had left for life in the military. With his tail between his legs, he stayed true to his lonely, stubborn path.

Soon after Tom left home, my mother turned to drinking and cigarettes to fill the lonely hours by herself. As a stroke survivor on a cocktail of medicines, it was strongly advised not to smoke or drink excessively, the last I knew it was strongly advised not to do these regardless of your medical condition! It's lucky enough she survived, let alone be able to partially walk and talk again. The hard work that two hospitals and countless staff had put into her recovery was being undermined by her insistent desire to fill her life with toxins not just on an enjoyable, moderate level, but on a level that had started to spiral into an out of control addiction.

One afternoon, she called me and asked if I would take her back home as she had been at a friend's house. It was clear she had been drinking from the tone of her voice. It took a lot of concentration for her to speak clearly, but impaired with alcohol this task became almost impossible. An afternoon of drink too would have also meant she could have made good progress into a pack of cigarettes. I would usually leave work early and plan my day around taking her to hospital for check-ups or trips out around our town, but on this occasion, I refused to take her home to make it clear I would have no part in her drinking or smoking. As an adult, she has every right to drink and smoke as much as she would like, but then again pouring these toxins into her body the way she did was a big step backwards for all the steps forward we were trying to take together for her health. She then called Tom to come and pick her up and he decided that he would take her home and condoned the fact I refused to pick her up, discounting the fact she had been blind drunk. He professed to her that from that day on if he saw me again he would, in his words, "kill me".

Threats are generally a real last chance method use by weak and insecure people to control what little hold they have left. In some cases, the threat of domestic violence can become a real eventuality and fatalities are painfully common in our society. A UK census conducted in 2017 reveals that one woman is killed every three days due to domestic violence. This striking data is part of the Femicide Census of the same year, of which 1.2 million women claimed to be victims of domestic abuse. The most saddening thing about these statistics is that the data gathered is only from only reported incidents and comprise mainly of offences that are punishable, such as emotional and physical abuse. How many more men, women and children are suffering at the hands of aggressive, manipulative partners in silence? How many will be subjected to abuse that doesn't leave the same marks as physical assault, but does leave deep emotional and mental scars?

After having experienced his exaggerations before, I again called his bluff and would do everything I could from then on for him to notice me. I would open the car door for her every time he came to pick her up and would say hello to him from the passenger door, yet he still chose to ignore me. It would seem for now that our conflict had terminated in his desperate attempt at threatening me. Again, his scheme backfired, leaving him looking like a fool who fell far short of every promise of retribution he made. It's safe to say Tom saw me many times after his threat but never did manage to kill me.

Lessons from Judgement and Intuition

"Never pretend to a love which you do not actually feel, for love is not ours to command." – Alan Watts

Belief

Belief in yourself or in something outside of yourself can be experienced and adopted as your understanding of a subject through many various ways. The most influential of these ways, through my experience, is through the opinion of someone else. Someone else's opinion of you can give you the power to grow into the person they tell you that you are, but unfortunately, they more commonly tell you that you aren't or can't be. When we adopt someone else's outside understanding of who we are, you are putting their opinion of you over your own opinion of yourself. Of course, you know more about yourself than anyone else on earth, but what you *think* you know about yourself differs greatly depending on who's influence you have fallen upon. While I don't believe there is an exact formula for everyone to follow so they can master self-belief, I feel it is my duty as someone comfortable with the subject to instruct you to never put someone else's opinion of you over your own opinion of yourself, unless they are seeking to help you. Baring this in mind, it is important to understand that while your esteem may be low, you can still easily ignore the opinions of other people by applying the aforementioned steps in previous chapters explaining how you should treat the dialog or opinions between you and your spiteful naysayers.

If your esteem is low, firstly find the courage to banish the voices of others who wish to belittle you further than you have done so to yourself already. You can then identify the abilities in your personality, achievements or other areas of your life that you know are strong and powerful. With these areas in mind, you can begin to advance towards your intensions with your identity in your own hands, never allowing another person to poke or prod at it uninvited. With only your best qualities in mind, you create for yourself an image of strength and align honestly with your individual, unique power. On your journey to self-belief or simply believing in a better way, a better life, if you allow the opinions of others to be the foundation you build your kingdom upon, you cannot be surprised when your walls collapse under such weak footings.

Allowing the self-belief of your own best abilities to be at the forefront of your ambition starts with the habits that you form every day. Belief isn't a gift or something that you are born with, it is a trait nurtured and grown by even the biggest and best personalities on Earth. Admiral McRaven, a retired US Special forces commander, presents the perfect case for achievement of your goals in his book 'Make Your Bed'. McRaven urges us to program our minds for success and achievement by starting as you mean to go on and create a small victory as the first act of the day – making your bed! While it doesn't exactly achieve world peace, it does gear one of the first cognitions of your brain as you awake to thoughts of success, as it is a very achievable task. When embarking on this book, my first endeavour at a manuscript dictating my personal philosophies, I was incredibly daunted with the prospect of hours of typing, editing and scrabbling for words to put together. When I asked my dear friend Emma how on Earth I was to complete this, she asked me "How do I eat an elephant?" I thought I'd start by asking if she had some ketchup, but that wasn't the answer. The answer was a simple, "one mouthful at a time", and that thought has been applied to this book or the multitude of other difficult undertakings I manage in my life. Thank you, Emma. Self-belief is also experienced in small mouthfuls until a larger meal of courage is consumed, and that full stomach feeling is your utter confidence. What you believe in and that which you know to be a truth in your life is undeniably your factual understanding of what it means to be you.

How do you achieve belief in yourself? One small victory at a time. Push those victories to the front of your mind and allow them to become your armour. Protected by the knowledge of your own abilities and prior successes, you will be impervious to the opinions of others. Your knowledge and opinion of yourself is your bedrock, not someone else's assumptions.

Get Curious

Sometime in my life, I grew a feeling of discomfort when faced with large open water. As a child I was a great swimmer, attending swimming clubs, spending all summer holidays snorkelling in the Red Sea or Mediterranean, surrounded by corals and tropical fish. Somehow, I had closed the door on my joy for the water and adopted a quiet fear and profound dislike to swimming in open water, but I cannot understand where it came from.

My other half, Chiara, grew up next to the Mediterranean Sea. She played so much in the water that she feels she may actually be a mermaid that didn't quite make it through her development enough to grow a tail… yet. She loves getting into the water and going beyond the breakers, out to where her features from the shore are indistinguishable. I, on the other hand, would wade out to my knees and stand there uncomfortably until she would return some thirty minutes later, elated at her exercise, panting and smiling wide in her watery element. Standing in the shallows, itching with discomfort because of some unknown fear that has crept up on me really didn't seem to fit my outgoing, courageous character. "I *have* to get over this" was my initial thought. I quickly grasped that the waters in front of me weren't physically holding me back, it was soft and gentle, and lots of people were playing and splashing in its beauty. Plus, if she could go out there without any problems, and I'm at least as fit as she is, then I must be able to do so too. The only difference between us both was that she knew she could swim and really benefit from the liberation of the sea, and I didn't want to believe that I could.

It wasn't the water itself that I feared, but somehow, I feared the feeling of facing my fear! I didn't know why I didn't like the sea, big, deep pools or any fast-flowing water including water rides, I hadn't even given it a thought because I was so content with my legs planted on the land. It may seem counter-intuitive then, to suggest this fear is exactly what I used to get over my dislike of the water. I started to cultivate a feeling of wonderment as to what it was that I didn't like so much until curiosity was a more powerful feeling than the fear itself. I suspended my irregular judgement, strode into the water, aimed at a small, orange buoy two-hundred and fifty meters away and I set off using breaststroke, gradually edging nearer towards it.

It was approaching the evening, and the sky began to shift from light blue into an orangey-pink. The water was tinted beautifully as the light reflected off the countless calm ripples surrounding me. With my head low in the water, dedicating my body to the strokes, the buoy seemed to get no closer to me even though my heart was working hard. I had finally advanced almost half the distance between the shore and my orange buoy, but my mind was still fighting the urge to scream and have my phobia take control, eventually drowning me.

Fifty meters away from the beach, voices from the shore gave way to a gentle lull of water against my skin and the occasional sound of my misplaced hand or foot breaking the surface of the water. One-hundred meters away from the beach, and my swim became more natural, the passing bits of seaweed which minutes beforehand I had mistaken for a hungry shark or great sea beast come to devour me had become a normal sensation, and I adopted the feeling as a reminder that gentle grasses and plants lived here too as much as they did on the land. A school of fish swam beneath me as if to cheer on the wimpy kid taking on his sea monster. While I thought the water here would be colder, I found warmth surrounding me from the solar-charged currents heated all day by the sun. Just meters away from my waypoint, my heart turned inwards, and butterflies fluttered throughout my body. A new sense of discomfort struck me, but it wasn't a fear of the endless sea around me. I was experiencing a sense of sadness as once I had reached the buoy, I would have to swim back to shore and leave behind the beautiful tranquillity I had found myself immersed in. I had faced my fear by swimming curiously into what I had always thought of as a great, scary abyss.

In all the time I stood knee deep in terror of the sea, I had also held myself back from its abundant beauty and serenity which I had discovered in the isolated splendour of my sunset swim. Now at the buoy, I tentatively let my feet down into the cooler water below. A clearly distinguishable cold met my toes and I quickly raised my legs again to tread water, scared of what lurked in the cold depths below. It was a similar feeling as when your foot is exposed from the duvet and a childlike fear sweeps through your mind as you imagine all sorts of monsters from under your bed snatching you by the foot! Armed with my new desire to explore my fears, I calmed my nerves and dropped my legs to the cool water below. I closed my eyes and placed my head back to rest in the sea's buoyancy. Breathing in the setting sun, I allowed my body and thoughts to slip away with the natural divinity of my watery setting.

Having faced my small but limiting fear, I unlocked a powerful energy and feelings of elation that I had not experienced before while my feet had been landlocked. Freeing up my fear and exchanging it for curiosity banished a limiting physicality in my life and I gained the incredible knowledge that when you become curious with their displeasure in something or someone, the most remarkable feelings can arise. My sea monster wasn't so much as a beast lurking beneath the waves of the ocean, it was a monster inside of me who I had given a home beneath the waves of my own subconscious thinking. Like a hero in a Greek epic, armed only with curiosity, I split the waters and found the monster to be a creation of my own thinking. For all the beasts you find lurking in your waters, jungles or deserts in your life, approach them with curiosity. Be it a relationship you are struggling to commit to or repair, a skill you are scared of mastering or physical endeavour you dread, get curious with it. Find out which element it is of your fear that makes you the most uneasy and work towards overcoming it any way you find easiest.

This same curiosity is what arose in me when trying to interpret my intuition. While I knew leaving home would be full of discomfort, I was curious to see how the truth may be discovered in my bold action. Though I don't recommend becoming homeless in pursuit of your curiosity, I do think that approaching a circumstance you are uneasy about with curiosity and courage will give you a strong sense of dependence on your own ability to sense right and wrong through the interpretation of your intuition. While my example demonstrates how I overcame my trepidation, you may find that you are out of reach of such success. You will, however, discover what is necessary to avoid or banish from your life to limit the amount of anxiety you face. You may not find yourself in a meditative state of bliss once you face your challenge, but you will certainly gain more experience with who you are and why you are the way you are. Only then can you overcome the task at hand and all discomforts you will find over the course of your time on Earth.

Practice

Life affords us many opportunities to practice and keep honed our intuition and self-belief. Though sometimes this can be experienced in times of suffering, it can also aid us in our self-betterment and strengthen our character. Practicing the letting go of our egotistical, boastful nature that is usually the standard setting for many people is the best way to access and listen to that small voice inside that will be our ultimate guide through our rough seas.

When a lesson has been learned through the various twists and turns in life, we understand a little more about what it takes to dedicate and commit ourselves to living a harmonious life. While the Christian may listen to scriptures and then read them all over again that same night, so too must we practice listening to our intuition to establish why these thoughts and feelings have arisen and what it is they are directing us to. Whether our intuition has come to speak to us as a friend, guiding us gently towards new horizons, or a drill instructor commanding us to move quickly away from a potentially dangerous situation, as we listen to it more and more each day we find a comfortable trust within its instruction. Sometimes, as I have found when listening to my intuition, the result of trusting that feeling inside isn't apparent at first. On these occasions, shutting yourself down and wishing you hadn't had acted on gut instinct or impulse will cause you to be blind to the eventual result. The more we listen to our intuition and understand its guidance, the louder and more profound it becomes until you reach a place where the entire shape of your life and all occurrences within it have been created through a steady appreciation of trusting yourself.

Practice curiosity within your life and seek to find answers for all things you don't fully understand. It is my belief that the real depth and constitution of all things is mysterious and may never be fully understood by mankind, but always seek to find answers to your questions, no matter how ambitious, in the most complete way. In my experience, this is how we further develop our understanding of self and relation to others. It is what leads us onwards towards other questions and other fulfilments in life while on the path to peace. Other than parental and societal influences, the inner desire that emerges from a child to want to become a spaceman, train driver or beauty therapist comes from a place totally immeasurable to science. The curiosity a child has to want to explore everything about what they want to be when they grow up then matures into what we call intuition, eventually seeking answers and success as they practice their independence. Often, this is how a childhood dream is achieved.

Through constant practice in a deliberate attempt to understand our intuition, we must think as a child does, defy our challengers and stay strong on the path we wish to travel. Practice again and again and restore your mind to the way it was in your childhood when hills were made for going fast down, walls were made to be climbed and hearts desires followed as wide and far as they would go. As Wayne Dyer has said, 'If prayer is you speaking to God, intuition is god speaking to you'. I believe this is what Matthew is alluding to in the bible verse 18:3, "unless you change and become like little children, you will never enter the kingdom of heaven."

Practice what you did so well at as a child, question everything and truly seek to understand everything about the situations you find yourself in.

97

Practice listening to and trusting your intuition and allow curiosity to grow inside you every day. Do this, and you will start to enter the gates of your own heaven.

Rejection to Adoption

"Why is it," Jonathan puzzled, "that the hardest thing in the world is to convince a bird that he is free, and that he can prove it for himself if he'd spend a little time practicing? Why should that be so hard?" - Jonathan Livingston Seagull, Richard Bach

The end of January 2014 arrived, so too had the time come to harvest the years of work I had put into my self-development and survival through countless tough obstacles. Now embarking on my military service, not only had I achieved a personal goal, but I had also won my ticket out of the misery of a broken home. I had signed up for a minimum four year service as an enlisted airman. This wasn't my first choice, but due to the budget cuts at the time and the closing of applications for the aircrew position I was seeking, this would be a way to experience life as a regular airman before my intention of internally transferring once the positions I wanted opened up again. The path ahead of me was clear, and from the outset of my career, I made plans to retrain to be an officer after a period of time, firstly learning to follow and develop an understanding of what I thought a good officer was before being in a strongly scrutinised position of leadership.

My last couple of days of civilian life were spent with my so-called adopted mum Samantha, my much loved best friend and their dad. I had this short period of time to think of how much experience I gained in such a short space of time. When I was sixteen, I'd become so very bitter with the world during my parent's painful divorce. I had been guided by an unknown understanding that flowed through all life and through all places. The lessons learned through this suffering taught me how I needed to think and feel in order to overcome or just get through situations with Tom, exercising silent caution and trusting my intuition. From witnessing the decreasing health of my mother and caring for her no matter how much she had turned her back on me, always loving her regardless of the pain she had inflicted upon me became my most treasured lesson. It demonstrated to me that loving your closest family members who hurt you the most is the only way to enjoy a truly serendipitous, peaceful life when we choose to interpret hardships as a way to grow. I was grateful for what I had become and ready to turn the page and move on.

I was just three weeks into training when I received a phone call from a debt collecting agency regarding unpaid fines dating back to the house they had rented in the months she had been in hospital. Unable to do anything about it from RAF Halton, I had to leave a message with my sisters to sort out the problem. It transpired that while she had been in hospital, Tom hadn't paid a number of energy bills and the court had come knocking to deliver the bad news – he had to pay up! I thought that in my absence, my mother's life would consist of her living under the care of Tom and perhaps, while he was very controlling, she would find comfort in the knowledge he would look after her indefinitely. I was struck with worry and fear and felt embarrassed that I believed if I removed myself from their life, she would live happily ever after. It was clear that there would be a long journey ahead of me to free myself of the reoccurring problems left over from the last three years that were following me.

Looking back to then, I struggle to see how I didn't have a total collapse of self-esteem or even a complete mental break down. Going through enormous pressure during my pre-RAF service, to the tiresome strain of training should have brought home the realisation that my family conditions and my own mental health, though I had patched it up, was terrible. I can only attribute my unwavering determination to get away from the life of disability, homelessness, sofa surfing and domestic trouble to how tough I had become in order to remain at a functioning standard, both physically and mentally.

Somehow, I had turned all the negative energy I encountered into a protective outer layer. Like a physical wound covered up without being cleaned and sterilised, my mental health wouldn't heal under that layer I had built up over many years. My identity became that of a person who had suffered in tough situations, a young man who only knew how to react and survive. Worse still, I was proud of my ability to suffer and attracted suffering into my life frequently. Habitually, I would encounter more and more trouble with domestic matters. I would literally think myself into troublesome situations, as I only identified with and responded to grief.

It's easy to step back now and ask myself what was I thinking? Why didn't I leave? Why did I antagonise situations, when I could have totally removed myself from the problems? It certainly is easy to think these things now, but back then I wasn't just a witness to my problems, I truly believed I had to be a part of them, I *was* them, and they were a part of me. I knew no other existence in those days than that of struggle and hardship. The outer shell I built for myself kept me alive and brought me this far, but as you'll see in a later chapter, this shell was fragile.

I graduated from RAF Halton's Recruit Training School on the 1st of April 2014. It was two years to the day that I had been woken up by Tom telling me of my mums sudden and violent stroke. As if the 1st of April 2012 initiated me into a deeply disturbed two years, April 1st 2014 was to initiate me into a four year struggle with mental health as the growing mess of rotten emotions would outgrow its prison, rise to the surface, and lead me to suicide. Somewhere along the journey I would now be taking, I would rediscover my inner harmony and most importantly my buddy, Bandit!

After graduation, I had a few days of leave to use before being shipped out of RAF Halton to start my second phase of training at the infamous DST Leconfield, a training camp run by the army in Yorkshire. During this time off I went to check up on my mother. She told me that Tom had briefly moved back in but had left the house once again. Feeling exhausted by the constant comings and goings of the man, and the fact that I didn't want to get involved with their relationship again, I didn't want to know the reasons why he had left. It was her business.

I spent the night at her house, and arranged that evening to take the dog, Dusty, to my father's that following afternoon for just a couple of days. Dusty was our adored family dog, and during their separation, he remained with my mother while my father was finding a place to live. When he had settled down Dusty was to go and live with him, but it was decided that due to my dad's small space on his narrowboat, it was best that the dog remained with her. The sudden change of her health had made it impossible to look after the dog properly, but as Tom grew fond of Dusty, he took it upon himself to care for the dog as if it was his own. Discovering the following morning that I was taking Dusty away for a weekend while I visited my dad, Tom flew into a rage.

***

The morning of the fight, I woke and heard my mother leaving the front door. I was only wearing my boxers when I got out of bed to look through the window to see if she had managed to walk to the car safely without falling over. As she got in the car, a few moments past before he switched the engine off. The driver door swung open and out stepped Tom in a frantic rage, red and sweaty. As he began to stride over to the house, it was very clear a conflict was about to occur, so I raced downstairs to the front door, still only dressed in my underwear, and prepared myself accordingly in physical demeanour and mental calmness. The familiar rattle of a key sliding through the metal barrel lock of the PVC door signalled that an appointment between him and I had been made, and the man who had wanted to 'kill me' might soon be in a position to do so, if he could. A heavy clunk downwards with the bulky handle and the door burst open with a force that rattled the frame as the capabilities of the hinges became compromised. In silent confidence, a six-foot-four, skinny as a rake, teenaged Charlie stood wearing nothing more than his pants in front of the visibly enraged Tom!

103

"I've come to take the dog." Tom barked his orders at me while his eyes scanned around to see if the dog was within reachingdistance of him. Embracing the power of my boxers, I stood firmly in nude defiance and told him that Dusty was to be taken to my dad's. In fact, the plan had now changed, my dad was driving over to collect the dog, though I didn't draw Tom to the fact that within five minutes my re-enforcements would arrive. He grabbed me by the arms and tried to pull me away from the position in front of the doorway, but I refused to move, not to restrict him from entering the house, but to make a clear statement that he could not bully me forever. If a fight was to be had to confirm my unwavering defiance of his cruel regime over the last few years, then unfortunately for him that is what he would get.

He fired the same old weak warning shots, yelling "don't mess with me, boy", but it was clear that I was making my stand and was ready to sort him out. He quickly snatched my throat with one hand, a familiar habit of his, the other raised in a fist to shoulder height, ready to strike a blow to my face. Swiftly, I changed my footing and allowed the force he was pushing against me to put his whole upper body in an off-balanced stance. I raised my hands to his shoulders and grabbed the silky fabric of his tracksuit jacket, though I didn't do any throat grabbing, that truly is a coward's move. He drew his fist back further, allowing me time to anticipate the blow, and brought it down on my cheek. In the precious moment that I knew the strike was coming, I pulled him towards me and to the left, dodging my head to the side, thankfully only connecting with his fist by a glance below my eye. Using his forward momentum, I swung him around one hundred and eighty degrees, pulling him through the doorway and knocking the shabby sheik

104

picture frame that hung on the wall, sending it crashing to the ground. With Tom now unsteady, I pushed forward and he fell onto the brown leather seat occupying a corner of the hallway. His hand had fallen away from me and so to had all his burning rage which now had been replaced with deep embarrassment and the certain look of a man who has realised he just made a mistake. He looked embarrassed as I dominated his attack by simply using his undisciplined aggression to topple him. Proud of my quick acting and non-violent reaction, I told Tom with confident grandeur he needed to calm down. A new wave of anger washed over him as my provocative comment unsurprisingly escalated the situation. Now grabbing me with two arms firmly around my waist, he rushed from his seat and attempted to wrestle me to the ground. I'm a skinny guy now, so back then I must have been almost toothpick snappable! It's a miracle I wasn't taken down to the ground at this point, but somehow I managed to handle a man much heavier than me into an almost defeated situation. What happened next isn't just a miracle, it was comedy gold!

It was a bank holiday, and many of the neighbours in the little suburban cul-de-sac were out gardening and cleaning their cars, so when they heard the fight in the hallway (the door was wide open still) everyone stopped to see if they could make out what was going on. It must have been a shock to then see a skinny, pale kid wearing nothing but his boxers, pick up a middle-aged man, one hand holding his collar, the other holding the belt of his trousers. Then, with a mighty effort, the skinny kid throws out the man like a bag of rubbish, onto the front garden! Better still was the crescendo of clattering glass, resembling pins split by a bowling ball, as the fray had knocked over the glass bottles left by the door, destined for the recycling bin.

I had somewhere inside of me summoned the strength to combat the menace of my youth and make a clear statement – I wasn't taking it anymore. I followed Tom outside and pinned him to the ground to refuse him any further chance of an attack on me. The neighbours watched and all but cheered for the violent display as if my mother's front garden had been an arena built by Rome, and they were the cheering mob of toga-clad citizens, thumbs pointed downwards urging me to finish him once and for all. I kindly asked Tom if he'd had enough, and when his answer was established through his muffled words (his face was in the grass), I let him get up. He stormed off, sulking and embarrassed towards the car where my mother waited. He stationed himself behind the steering wheel and started the engine. Assuming he was going to drive off, I walked towards the car to catch my mother's attention and tell her I was okay. She held her head in her hands, and when she saw me she cried, shaking her head slowly, mouthing, "I'm so sorry."

Assuming my walk towards the car was a threat, Tom got out a second time, took off his jacket and asked me if I "wanted some more". I didn't react with anger or even take a defensive stance, I simply wondered what on Earth he was talking about. His only connecting punch had barely registered a mark on my face and all other punches he threw at me during his pathetic wrestle fell far short of the mark, ending him up in a heap on the grass, with me, Gollum like in my pants, perched on top of him. I would never brag about winning a fight, as I believe breaching someone's peace by means of physically reprimanding them is an incredible violation unless in a situation where you were first attacked or you are defending another, but it was clear that I was not the loser. You can ask the neighbours who witnessed the conflict while watering their Geraniums, trimming their hedges and sweeping their front doorsteps! I told Tom to leave, reminding him that he'd been embarrassed enough for one day. He returned to the car and wheel spun away, leaving the dog to slumber, the neighbours to dream of gladiatorial splendour and me standing in semi-naked majesty, mouth open in bewilderment over what had just happened.

I ran back inside the house and put on some clothes. I was convinced that Tom would return, so protecting both myself and my mother, I decided to report the incident to the police. I was squeaky clean out of RAF training and convinced myself that if Tom had decided to report what had happened as an assault that I had initiated, I would be in real trouble. Outside, I heard the low rumble of his car pull up again, followed closely behind by my dad's old Citroen Berlingo. I opened the door to an animated argument as Tom told my dad what he thought of me, and according to him, my dad's inability to raise a child. I went to Tom's car as their argument intensified and asked my mother if she was okay. She was shaken and confused and didn't respond to anything I said. A few moments later a police car turned up. I introduced myself as the caller, then the officers questioned Tom and I individually. While being asked by the officer to come with him, Tom lashed out and refused to cooperate, causing the officer to assert his wishes upon him, and with a forceful, guiding hand, Tom was marched by the policeman around the corner to cool off. The whole scene was embarrassing. An easily avoidable situation was turned into, yet again, a dramatic domestic issue, caused and escalated by Tom determined to illustrate that only his way was good enough. But damn, what a good show it must have been for the neighbours!

While on the subject of physical violence, this is a great place in this book to talk about the principle of turning the other cheek. This principle has an important part to play in our society and all humans in order to reach out to others from a higher, peaceful position. However, physical harm should only be used in circumstances where you or someone else is in imminent threat of harm or are being subjected at that moment to an attack. No child or adult should be taught that sending positive vibes and hugging trees is the way to deal with a physical violation of your rights, after all, humans were equipped with pain receptors for a reason, and to smile through a barrage of punches while thinking "it's okay, it's just the way they were raised" is clearly ludicrous. To understand why, how and when physical intervention is needed, I now bring your attention back to the Tao. Read these wise words from verse 31 from the Tao Te Cheng. It captures the idea of how physical violence should be reacted to and how you should conduct yourself in times where you deem physical force necessary;

"He enters a battle gravely,
with sorrow and with great compassion,
as if he were attending a funeral."

Humble defiance is a masterful art, for you cannot fight someone who doesn't want to fight you. I'd like to include here the Alan Watts

108

edition of the 'No Sword School' samurai story. The story follows one of Japan's greatest samurais', Miyamoto Musashi, who not only was trained so well with a sword but also trained in the art of Zen.

"There was a very great Samurai—no less than Miyamoto Musashi. He was taking a ferry boat across Lake Biwa, which is the great lute-shaped lake north of Kyoto. After he had gotten on the boat, suddenly a drunken Samurai came bouncing aboard. He looked at Miyamoto and said, "Ha! I see you're a Samurai. What's your school?"

He [Miyamoto] said, "A no sword school."

He [Drunken Samurai] said, "Hahaha." (The boat had taken off by this time and was going across the water.) "No sword school. What a thing. What a thing. I'll try out your no sword school." (and he drew his sword) "Come on!"

Miyamoto said, "No, no, no. Wait a minute, there are a lot of people around on this boat and if we start fighting, somebody might get hurt. Why don't we go over to that island there, and we can fight there."

So he said to the ferryman, "Row over to that island."

So they went over to the island and this drunken samurai was all ready to get into a fight and he jumped off the boat onto the island and quickly Miyamoto grabbed the oar from the ferryman and pushed the boat out into the water and left him [Drunken Samurai] stranded there.

He [Miyamoto] said, "You see my no sword school."

This approach to necessary violence to stop a breach of your harmony, or if you are acting to defend the harmony of someone else, comes from the simple knowledge that our enemies are human too, with their own upbringing, code of morals, understanding of right and wrong, and the truths of their own life, no matter how destructively they are acting. What compassionate, conscious, intellectual person would want to eagerly end or harm the life of another human being when they know their assailant is truly reacting to how they have been taught to react given the conditions of their life? My mind is drawn to the Native American proverb, "No tree has branches so foolish as to fight amongst themselves."

When the police had calmed Tom and the stupidity of our conflict was realised, the police became placid and started taking statements from us both. During this time, my mother took herself out of the car, limped her

110

way past me and went immediately to Tom's side, hugging him and pampering him. I didn't ask for any sympathy from her, but after seeing her tell me that she was sorry when I approached the car previously, I assumed she felt I deserved sympathy. Tom had instigated a fight with her own son, but now she was comforting him, not even stopping to ask if I was okay after having been punched in the face. The moment she arrived by his side, he became very pitiable and soft why she consoled him, adding to my frustration.

The hardest fact of life is that the people who undermine your feelings most likely are those closest to you. Whether or not this is because they are the ones you spend most of your time with or because they are most likely to have a strong influence on you is irrelevant. Being downtrodden by a person you let into your life or are intrinsically part of your life, sucks.

Human beings are uncomfortable when challenge or change comes their way, and the simplest response will be that of stress, which to some people can take irrational and aggressive forms. Learning to understand the best way to react to someone's upset is crucial to your bliss and guiltless existence, which I believe we are here to enjoy and have a right to. I'm not suggesting for you to tread carefully around those you may upset as if not delivering the truth is the best answer, but always seek to confront the situation using the right timing and environment. Your attitude and speech should always come from a place of love and respect so that they can be guided by your calm to help them to meet you on a higher ground where compassionate conversations can be had. Before a conflict can be initiated, try with every effort to first communicate your feeling with them during a sacred time set aside only for them, such as the dinner table, after a pint at the pub, or during a stroll through the local park or countryside. Speak to people in person, face to face, where the sincerity and tone of the conversation can be monitored and perfectly delivered. Holding their hand, embracing or maintaining eye contact also denotes the sincerity of how you approach the topic. Of course, the magnitude of the person's aggressiveness or the imminence of the situation may render it impossible to have a pink and fluffy, touchy-feely conversation. In these instances, find the courage to speak to them from your inner peace and act from inner strength. Simply allow the comments of your oppressor to wash over you and remind them that you are unwilling to accept their opinions as your own. Find the courage to understand the lessons in their words and actions, but leave their negativity with them, don't take it with you.

Had I have seen this situation coming, perhaps I too could have avoided the aggressive clash and the subsequent conversation with my mother. The police returned to their vehicle and Tom sat back in the driver seat of his car. I spoke to her about what had happened, and why she had done nothing to prevent Tom acting the way he did, and why after the fight she had hadn't said a word to me, instead only comforting my assailant. She shook her head again and could only tell me she was sorry. I let her know that seeing her was a bad idea and I couldn't stay at home with her again. We walked to the car and I said goodbye, knowing we both needed to cool off from this situation and would likely not see each other again for a while.

***

Months of my initial military life passed as I settled into my role as an airman based at RAF Coningsby, Lincolnshire. For the first time since I was 15, I had a settled job, a clear career path, and had physically and emotionally slipped the shackles of my former life. I was a young man with lots of responsibilities, a steady income with a huge amount of other benefits and a sense of enormous pride for the character I had become through the situations I had endured. The red-blooded, egocentric young man in me had finally sprung forth, and I seemed to forget I owed everything I had become to the hard times that formed me and the lessons that came with them which had previously humbled me. Though I didn't go and see her too often, I knew from what my sisters had told me that my mother's condition was mysteriously worsening, and her ability to conduct herself physically and mentally was ebbing away. She was also left alone with Tom who came in and out of her life, which troubled me immensely as I couldn't be there to look after her and my sisters who were both hundreds of miles away, one choosing a life in a foreign country. Though our relationship had been patched after I chose to leave home, adopting a life in transient homelessness in woodlands and on sofas, it was decided between us that in order for her to live peacefully I should have very little to do with her. That decision we had reached hurt me deeply inside as once again I had to step away from her because of the man who had plagued my teenage years.

One day my sister called me to stress how sorry for me she was about the cat. I had no idea what she was talking about, so she apologised profusely and was shocked that I hadn't been told. Without my knowledge, my loyal companion through childhood, Socks the cat, my friend since my 6th birthday, was put down after having difficulty standing. It was suspected that a head injury may have triggered an accumulation of biological shutdowns that led her to suffer before the decision was made to have her put to sleep. Prior to this, Tom had tried to uproot my mother from the house they once lived in, but the new house he wanted to rent for them both didn't accept cats. With the son warned off, the cat gone and a new home for them both, my relationship with my mother was almost completely extinguished. Tom never did like my cat much and though I cannot comment on what happened in the last days of her life, I have dreadful opinions on what had caused my cat's head injury.

I drove home on Christmas leave, 2014, to enjoy a marvellous time with my adopted mum, her amazing family and of course the sofa I called my bed. I had slept on that sofa on and off for a year now from before I started training and after while on leave, or at weekends away from the airbase. The sofa, while it didn't accommodate my six foot and four inch length, was the cosiest bed I had enjoyed for years. It wasn't the sofa that was incredible, it was upholstered in cream leather and would stick to me throughout the night and have to be peeled off my back in the morning, but it was the home the sofa occupied that was so fantastic. Had I not been loved and cared for by Samantha and her family I would have become desperate and demotivated. My friend and I would stay up until stupid o'clock playing games, drinking beer and eating Doritos, and I felt that my place was amongst them, not just as a guest, but a truly valued member of a functioning family. She would kiss my head, say "God bless, don't stay up too late or you'll get red eyes", then she'd wander up to bed.

I believe that of all the people I have loved, family or otherwise, Samantha truly gave me the strength of purpose to realise my failings and the failings of others were only here to test me, to prepare me and guide me further through our journey as human beings. Though she was often angry at the circumstances and events of my life, she always did believe that God's plan was great and totally unbiased. In her opinion, he moved in mysterious ways and was testing me on my road towards my higher purpose. Relying heavily on her unshakeable faith, she would tell me often how God has a plan for everyone and it's our responsibility to honour that plan, whichever way it would lead us. As if I couldn't feel more love for such a saintly woman, that Christmas she told me that their home was mine and I was now a son of hers. We had joked before about me being her adopted son, and I had heard her introduce me as her own boy on previous occasions, but I had always humbly shrugged these comments off with quiet gratitude. But this conversation had made it clear. Though the identity of my childhood family was no longer the same, their house, that sofa and the love they gave me was my sacred ground. I had found my people and I felt like I had a home once more.

Lessons from Rejection and Adoption

"Understanding is the first step to acceptance, and only with acceptance can there be recovery." — *J.K. Rowling*

Acceptance

Many friends and family members had offered me support during the time before my RAF service. People knew how complicated my home life was, even a former boss had offered me his place to stay in while I sorted my life out. I would always smile and be very grateful, but my inner pride and typical British 'stiff upper lip' always caused me to thank them and only let them know I was "okay, thank you." Often people would tell me that if I needed anywhere to go, I could always count on them, even if it was just for a cup of tea and a chat. I never did accept any of these offers to stay away from my troubled home life for a few days, or even pop round for a cup of tea! I felt it was my heroic mission to stay strong and show no one I had weaknesses or had failed at any part of my life, even when I spent time in homelessness.

Looking back, I was a fool not to accept the generosity and love of others. When I finally let Samantha take care of me as she too had been asking for a rather long time, I felt like the weight of the world had been

116

lifted off my shoulders. The effect that accepting love and generosity had on me was one of the few attributes that really gave my mental health problems a conclusive end (though we've not even begun to unravel that part of the story yet). Without learning this lesson early on, I may never have sought the help, kindness and love of others, both professionally and emotionally, who in later years I finally opened up to and allowed to be part of my healing process.

Accepting help isn't accepting defeat or weakness. Through my acceptance of help, I discovered how much fulfilment it gave to Samantha and her family. She told me that once I had settled into her home and I had escaped my problems, she too finally felt she could rest easily, knowing she was helping someone without any conditions, only wishing the very best for me. The joy in her life had raised when I accepted her proposal for help, and a small part of suffering she experienced when witnessing my problems lifted. At one point I was blamed for costing her so much money on getting her hair dyed, as she said the worries I gave her turned her hair grey! Seeing how putting my pride to once side had changed her life reinforced our relationship, I began to realise that countless other people had suffered while seeing me suffering too. Their pain could have been stifled by just opening up a little bit more, visiting them for tea and discussing with them my problems, and accepting that these people had come into my life to give me love. Perhaps my way of always striving to survive alone had conditioned me to believe that I couldn't bring my problems to anyone else, and thus I was weaker for not accepting help. When other people came around to support and give me love, I became stronger than ever.

You too will experience the same joyful feeling when you put aside your ego and allow others to come to your aid. You will begin naturally to then unpack your baggage, as love has no space for baggage, and joy is too light to be shackled by dramatic episodes of your past. You will learn to stop living in the past and move your full attention into moments of laughter which can only occur in the moment itself. Think about the funniest thing that you can ever remember and I'm certain you will mildly laugh to yourself, but I can guarantee you didn't laugh as hard as the moment the funny event took place, simply because living in the past is nowhere near as good as living in the moment. Bring yourself to accept the love of others, leave your baggage behind, and get ready to experience love, laughter and joy first hand in the very moment it happens. The best part is that the instant you start to accept help, you will release yourself from living in the past, and you'll find yourself living in the moment for as long as you choose to do so.

Moving On

The only logical step after accepting the help of all those who have come to your aid is to move on. When we move on, we don't leave behind the awful things that have happened to us, but we take the best from them and learn the lessons they have taught us. It is only under the influence of that positive energy from recycling our trouble that we can begin to step towards new, happier chapters in our lives. Identifying with the occurrences of your past is a way of living still in the past. So long as you identify as a suicide survivor, a fired employee or a failure to your spouse, you cannot begin to thoroughly advance towards a brighter future for yourself. Trying to move past terrible events with the mentality of a damaged person can only lead you into thought patterns *of* a damaged person, and, sooner or later, you will relive the same problems or create ones much worse.

Sometimes, as I experienced at the time, you will not find closure. There won't always be a blessing at the end to your experiences, and a lesson or purpose to your suffering may not reveal itself straight away, or perhaps ever. In that case, moving on can still be achieved, and the primary lesson we learn in these instances is to appreciate in yourself the strength of character it takes to walk away from certain roads in life and set our heading on easier, calmer streets. Moving on and accepting the absence of closure in life can be a wholly empowering event. Not requiring an answer and yet being able to grow from it and move towards a better life is the ego's greatest test. You may feel like you want to stomp your feet and demand that life gives you immediate answers for your plight even though you already know there is no direct answer that can be found. Surrendering, accepting, and moving on is the only way to forget the pain, and notice joy, love and abundance of support flowing so freely to you from your family, friends or whoever else you place your trust in. When you don't allow yourself to wholly move on, you place a big obstacle between you and your purpose on Earth which was bestowed upon you even before you arrived here. Let one of your greatest strengths become the knowledge that you are able to move on with your life and be happy, even when the answers from your painful past haven't presented themselves.

Growth

In the silent moments that I had to myself after Samantha and her family had gone to sleep, I could really start to reflect on the journey I had undergone. On the weekends, I would leave the RAF station and spend my two days off in their wonderful home, and every weekend I could finally switch off from my work and personal problems and notice in myself that I was growing in the comfort and security of my adopted family. I could begin to see how I had learned from a young age to be very prideful and always work my way out of my own problems, but this concept had also given me an inability to seek and accept help. Once I had accepted the help, I could see how moderate pride could motivate me to a degree, but only when I surrendered my ego and accepted the love of others could I truly see that I could outgrow any motivation that my pride bestowed upon me, not just to allow happiness to flow my way, but also to allow happiness to flow from me towards others.

I urge you to take time on a day that best suits you to reflect on your week, month and year. This can be achieved through meditation if you're comfortable with that, or in silent contemplation, which is a very similar thing. Assessing your understanding of yourself will bring with it a natural début of why you had to experience things the way you did. While enjoying this time, focus on the good lessons you have learned and the purpose of your struggle will start to explain itself to you. Aged nine I won a book from a traveling poet who I admired as if he was some kind of deity. I have always wanted to write a book and always seemed to radiate towards writing in school, doing very well in lots of essays. At fourteen I started writing a short sci-fi novel. While in the Air Force I was approached by the station commander to write for the RAF magazine. I didn't understand then, but my practice with writing helped me conjure this book together. Coupled with my suffering as a young man, I can now see that I couldn't have written all this information and strived to motivate and inspire other people without my growth through the trials I faced. I grew through difficulty, found an easier path and continue to grow with each day I write a new page, adding towards my confidence with writing and expressing my feelings and philosophy for other people.

Perhaps your redundancy was the necessary shove you needed in order to finally pursue your dream career. Maybe your boyfriend left you so that you may now travel and seek fulfilment far beyond what a lover could give you. In a world with endless inspiration, it really is how you view your conditions that allow you to judge how best to grow into the person you are supposed to be and who you want to be. Your thoughts and feelings can either nurture your soul and allow you to grow in a thousand ways, or they can keep you frozen and scared, never growing and remaining the same person you have been for years. Either way you see your circumstances, only you get to choose if you wish to use the past to help you grow or keep you in limbo. Just by reading this book and absorbing my encouraging words, you have stepped towards growth, and I think you're doing fantastic, so keep growing, and enjoy the journey you're on!

Obligation and Love

"Don't try to tell me what's on your mind,
The sorrow of having been left behind
Or the sorrow of having run away.
All that can wait for the light of day.
Meanwhile feel obligation-free;
Nobody has to confide in me." – Robert frost

This book has been written to inspire others through my own open experiences and perhaps give them hope for the situations they are in or have experienced, but it also serves to guide you towards understanding why I started the prolific adventures around the world with a very special animal. You may not think an animal with such short stature, long body, dense and sometimes smelly fur, packing an even more odorous personality would be an ample travel companion. While James Bond jets around the globe kicking ass and fighting crime with scantily clad glamour models on his arm, my companion wasn't so glamorous. Indiana Jones, Harry Potter and even Postman Pat had their share of company on their multitudes of adventures, from child sidekicks to cute and helpful animals, but my buddy and our relationship was more akin to Han Solo and his Wookie friend, Chewbacca! I am of course talking about one of the bestest friends our planet has yet afforded me – Bandit the ferret. My story so far has no benefit to me without the consolidation of hope that this animal brought to me. From here on in, my story becomes our story, and it begins on a country road in Lincolnshire on a frosty March morning of 2015.

I was ambling my way through the multitude of flat, straight country roads of rural Lincolnshire. Formally, Lincolnshire was the haunt of many of the UK's military heroes of the 20th century such as Lawrence of Arabia on his beloved motorbike, Guy Gibson and his fearless young aircrew who would give their lives to the defeat of the Nazi power in Europe, and many brave parachute regiment soldiers who too paid the ultimate price in one of Britain's most daring and disastrous operations in Arnhem, Holland. The county was full of historic pubs and airfields which I would visit on my days off, as I was fantastically stationed in the heart of 'Bomber County'.

One Sunday, in the mid-afternoon, I was returning from one such location driving my £400 bargain banger car through the white light of winter sun. By this time of year, a hairpin trigger had been set off in the seasons, and winter began to subside to its more virtuous of seasonal brethren, the spring. Though the end of winter was in sight, frost still danced in the shadows of the hedgerows. Occasionally, icy dancers were spun out too far from the shade into the suns lethargic gaze, melting their frozen waltz which fell as a wet layer among the tufts of grass on either side of the tarmac. The roads were narrow, but wide just enough to pass two cars between without too much hindrance to either driver, but when meeting with lorries or tractors you had to pull over to one side to let the larger, slower vehicle pass. The small engine of my little blue car gave a concerned change of pitch as I shifted from 5th to 3rd, slowing it's speed with the footbrake, preparing to take a familiar corner in this stretch of road. Usually, I would take the best line through the bend and accelerate through, testing the handling of the car, which surprisingly for an old machine was fantastic. This time, instead of putting my foot down on the accelerator until I could shift up to 4th and then 5th gear again on the straight, empty road ahead, I had to quickly come off the throttle and press hard on the brake. What looked like a sausage rolled out on the tarmac and sprinted in the direction I was heading in, as if it was racing me. Then, without hesitation, it cut in front of my car and I was certain it would meet it's death under the front tyre. Though I was slowing down fast, had the sausage not had legs and the speed of a thousand gazelles, it would have been brown bread! The quick sausage darted across the road, through the tufts of grass, over the frosted leaves and handed his fate to another death other than at the hands (or tyres) of my car. Owing to an upbringing in the woods and fields of rural Essex, I immediately knew this leg owning sausage was none other than one of the most elusive of the UK's mammals, a stoat!

I returned my hardy bargain car to the RAF station, still beaming from the encounter with the little mammal, and decided that my life had one tiny little hole in it that could be filled with a furry companion. The airbase didn't allow cats (though at one point I did look after a stray) and the rooms were too small for dogs. I looked into stoat ownership and realised for myself these little sausages were not commonly domestic, or even domesticable. My search for a stoat hindered, I turned to the most similar thing, *Mustela putorius furo* – Ferrets!

124

The next day I called the two people who would become the so-called grandparents of Bandit, and arranged to visit them and their small ferret rescue centre called New York Ferret Rescue, which I had unknowingly driven past almost every day in the six months of service as their garden backed onto the perimeter fence of the airbase. I was lulled into a sense of certainty by one of their old rescue girls, a jill (the correct name for a lady ferret) called Dolly. Dolly was blind and very placid, so my misconception of ferret behaviour grew from there!

The next day, certain that I could manage a calm, docile pet like a ferret (ha!), I made arrangements to see in the daylight all their available rescues in need of homes. Some fat boys (hobs to the well-read ferret handler) as big as cats were sniffing the air as I walked by their mismatched cages. Other smaller jills and hobs squabbled and ran wild, like whack a mole targets, through a large tree trunk that I was told they had made holes in themselves through dedicated, ferrety digging and nibbling. When the dozen or so ferrets saw me approach, some stopped and climbed the chicken wire of their large enclosure, exposing their fuzzy tummies to my perusal. Some nibbled my fingers, while some that I was encouraged to hold fell asleep in my arms. I was told that some adored the company of others and would not be separated, whereas a few, much different from all the others, preferred solitude. After all, they were all rescues and their experience with humans and other animals hadn't always been so peaceful.

With all colours considered, sizes, ages, backstories and habits, one smaller boy stood out. He didn't yet have a name, and he was rescued from the age of approximately one year old, but due to the condition of his teeth from his inappropriate housing in his time before entering the rescue centre it was difficult to age him accurately. He stood patiently and still, but with a boisterous look in his eye, his front paws slightly tilted inwards, lifting his head as if to ask aloud "who's this lanky bloke then?" He was picked up and set on the grass away from the other curious ferrets in the cage, some of who watched longingly as the chosen ferret ran and played in the foliage. He skulked up to a garden gnome, the noblest of backyard decorations, and knocked him off his guard, sending him toppling to the ground. The ferret turned to havoc, spooked by the collapse of the gnome and proceeded to dance and fling himself around the garden, taking on pots, upright shovels and other ferrets loose in the penned-in garden, who until being disturbed had been minding their own business.

"This is the one" I told the rescue centre owner and saviour of these naughty yet innocent little animals. I assured him this was to be the ferret that I would adopt and do all I could to give him the best life that he deserved, little did I know then how much of an incredible life we would have together. With all names considered, Bandit would be his most fitting title, though officially his name was 'The Bandit'. We arranged that I would collect Bandit in a weeks' time after I had secured permissions from the various offices and officers on the base that I needed to address before I could take up the responsibility of taking him into my life.

***

"HA HA HA!"

The station warrant officer crowed loudly through his rough voice, corse with years of shouting drill orders and disciplines across the length of the station. "THAT'S THE BEST ONE YET! HA HA HA!" He crowed again as I stood in his daunting, ancient office, festooned with framed photographs from his years of military service, bulging folders full of disciplinary documentation and other paraphernalia establishing his seniority and rank within the RAF.

I had only recently come out of training and was barely above the lowest rank in the air force. I was green as grass. Approaching the station warrant officer at this time in my career usually implied that I had dropped the ball and was being marched to his office for a stern telling off. But in order to have Bandit accepted as a member of the stations itinerary of pets owned by airmen and women, this was the final – and most important – signature I needed. I already had four signatures from my line manager, his boss, his bosses boss and the police section, all of which reacted with the same laughter and disbelief.

"WHO SENT YOU HERE?!" He barked again through a deep chuckle, assuming like the others before me I had been sent as a joke by an old senior friend to wind him up. He regarded me as a tradesman's apprentice, sent to get a jar of bubbles, a bucket of tartan paint, or a long wait.

"It's serious, sir, I would like to keep a ferret. I've already named him Bandit," and I handed him the paperwork. His comical reaction turned to disbelief and he put on his glasses to read the application, signed by four of the necessary referees already. He shook his head, asked for my name as we hadn't met before (thankfully, as that would usually mean I'd been a naughty boy), and he signed my paperwork. As he did, he shook his head and tutted with a smile, exclaiming in all his years he'd never known of a ferret kept on an airbase. With a warning to me that he was an animal lover and should any wrongdoing in Bandit's life be discovered, he would in his words, come down on me "like a ton of bricks", he signed and approved the paperwork. Assuring him I would look after my new friend, I stood to attention at his door, turned, and marched away.

The first day Bandit spent with me was the first time in his life that he truly had found someplace to put down his own small rucksack and sleep easy for the first night in a long time. Though he may not have known or believed it, this would be his forever home. He didn't have one physical place to call home, for he would see many countries, hotels, houses and tents, but his forever home would be my heart, bursting full of love and understanding for his needs. I too considered myself somewhat of a rescue, having been scooped up from the floor by Samantha's family after being kicked about like an unwanted pet. Not only did I feel immense gratitude at being rescued by my adopted family, but as you will see in these following pages, Bandit too had also come and unknowingly rescued me from fatal thoughts and feelings.

I wasted no time in slipping on a ferret harness around Bandit's head, arms and chest. I had my dad's old leather lead from his very first dog, which had been all our dog's leads' since. Now the baton had been passed to the first non-canine pet who was to walk further countless miles under its ancient guidance. The worn leather looked too robust and over the top to be used with such a small animal, but the extra patina we added to its appearance went to show how much usage and miles of walking we really did cover together, though neither of us was to know that in those early days. We walked together around the airbase every night after work and played all moments of the evening when Bandit wasn't asleep. Our walks graduated from gentle strolls across the station and soon my confidence and trust in Bandit grew, so we started towards more adventurous heights through woodlands, towns and beaches. While walking on the airbase, I would often be stopped by officers to question "what is it?!", and "what's its name?!" as you can imagine, we quickly grew a reputation.

One day I drove down to RAF Brize Norton to pick up a returning military policewoman. During the chit chat of the long journey, she asked me if I had "seen the ferret man". I pleasantly let her know that I saw him every single day first thing in the morning when I would shave in the mirror. It was true, we really had started to turn heads on base and around the local community, and much, much further. Sometimes we ventured into London to see my dad. With Bandit fast asleep in my pocket, it was really easy to sneak him into pubs to meet various interesting strangers, we even managed to walk around the British Museum together while he was asleep in my hoodie (Bandit that is, not my dad!) When you walk a ferret everywhere you go, you really do meet some unusually charming folk. While I loved walking Bandit (he clearly loved it too as he would beg at the door to go outside), I never did see our forays into the public as any kind of exhibition or showing off. I had a ferret shaped hole in my life which I had filled, and I wanted nothing more than to adventure with my new friend.

Every Friday Bandit was brought into my section and was often regarded as a mascot, though some of the personnel really didn't like him too much. My boss, a career man and warrant officer, would ask every time he saw me "where is the ferret?", and that I didn't have to leave him in my quarters, I could leave Bandit in his office throughout the day. Bandit also saw employment in the section bar, which for a time had problems with rats. A couple of days with the ferret in the bar and the reign of our resident rats was over. To my disappointment, the bar was from then on remembered unofficially as the 'Rat Trap', honouring our former pestilence, though I believe it should have been called 'The Thirsty Ferret' to credit Bandit, the saviour of the bar!

Bandit's place in my family grew too, being hailed as my dad's furry grandchild, and Samantha's little boy. He would travel down with me every weekend I spent at home, and tolerated long car journeys by either sitting up on the dashboard, curled up on my lap or even better, asleep the whole journey in his hammock I had made for him in a travel cage. If we were sat in traffic, I often would let him sit upon my shoulder, wind down the window and let him sniff the unusual air and listen to the strange sounds of traffic, attracting the attention of motorists as they crawled past, their mouths wide open in curious shock. My shoulder proved to be the best place for a ferret, as this was his lookout, his bed and his throne throughout the hours we spent together in the name of adventure until his very last days. I was very open-minded about how I kept Bandit. He had cages and his own space, but I found letting him free roam was the best option for us both. I could trust him to use the litter tray, not cause any damage to furniture or get himself into any other trouble. Though he had access to my bed, small sofa and clothing, I would usually find him asleep in his little hammock built into his cage. Restricting Bandit from things just made his curiosity run wild, becoming restless and grumpy until he sniffed at or climbed on whatever it was he wanted. Once he discovered how uninteresting it actually was, he would ignore it and never bother with it again.

Because of our near constant contact and my trust in him, and he in I, we had formed an incredible bond together. I could call him, and he would come running up to me, with a low, juddering chuckle known as dooking, which is the sound ferrets make of contentment, much like a cat's purr. Not only was it remarkable that I could call him and have him respond, he would also walk very long distances on his lead. Sometimes I could even trust him well enough to walk off his lead with me through woodlands, fields or quiet urban areas. When he wanted to come up and be held, observe the world from my shoulder or fall asleep in my jacket, he would paw at my trouser leg. If I didn't pick him up right away, he would climb up himself all the way to my collar, then squeeze down my top and fall asleep. Better still, I knew when it was time for him to use the little boy's room, a handy understanding when traveling far and wide so no accidents would occur! Having no prior experience with ferrets, I thought all these docile, domestic qualities to be common, but they most certainly were not. Bandit, the adventure-seeking, chilled out and friendly ferret was indeed special, though the true degree of his travelling potential would not be measured for some time.

***

Now many months had passed since the fight, I started to occasionally meet my mother back in Essex on the free weekends I had. Though I was working on my relationship with her, I limited these visits to protect my happiness and my poor mental health, which I knew was stirring just below the surface of the scar that my new life had helped me start forming. We met at high street coffee shops, as these became her Mecca during her last months of able-bodied movement. I would park and wait outside her new home in Southend-On-Sea, a property better suited to her ability as her condition worsened. I wasn't allowed access to the property on Tom's orders, though she did defy this quite regularly and let me inside briefly. On some occasions, she would even like to look after Bandit too, while I took Dusty the dog for walks. She had been visiting the hospital for new tests, as for some reason she had begun to fall more frequently, and her speech was failing. While several tests were carried out, no definitive answer as to the mysterious disability was found. It was painful to see her suffering so much, not just from the physical loss of her right side, her memory and speech, but also from the symptoms of this new and unknown disease.

Adding to the mix of suffering once again was Tom. He had taken control of the company accounts and refused to let her see them. She still had very little control of her money, and all personal accounts, letters and bills were managed by him. Her clothes were chosen by him, and the time she would try and spend out of the house was regulated, refusing to let her see certain friends and family. What is worse is the fact he would still go absent from their home without an explanation as to where he had gone. It was brought to my attention by her, though I cannot back up her claim, that police had been around to the house to speak to him regarding a visit by her speech therapist. The claim she made was that while the therapist was attending her, Tom came home and grew upset with the way he had told him he must take care of her. He was forced to the door of the house, and a blow was struck to the man who fell out the doorway onto the front garden path. Tom's side of the story, according to my mother, was that he got upset with the abusive therapist, who then fell out of the doorway as he left.

Observing her diminishing health and happiness on many occasions while living with Tom convinced me that something had to be done. I asked her the hardest question I had to face before, "was Tom abusing you?" She looked away sadly and confirmed with a nod. In a text message prior to this conversation between her and I, she now told me she had previously tried to explain this concern but couldn't find the words to express herself. Now knowing with certainty that she was being abused emotionally, financially, and mentally (we suspected physically too, though she never admitted it), it was time that matters were taken into our own hands. I raised the concern with my sister and we enlisted the help of my mother's gardener. We devised a plan to quickly and quietly relocate her into the care of an incredibly friendly, golden-hearted man who lived an hour away from her house while Tom was at work. He was a mutual friend of my parents, and after their divorce he grew a considerable fondness towards her and had even honourably asked my dad if he could take her on a date, to which he happily agreed. It was November 2015, and I had just three days until I would ship out for a four-month detachment to the Falkland Islands. I hurriedly received approval to borrow a work van and confirmed with my sister that our rescue mission should be set to go ahead that next day.

***

We set off early on a Friday morning in the borrowed van and I took the newest member of my section along for the ride, it was one of his days off and he volunteered to help me and my family. We arrived mid-morning and immediately begun to assess what needed to be taken away and what could be left there. With the very few things she had, it would take us very little time to fully pack her belongings into the van. My sister and the gardener arrived soon after, and with all hands on deck, the house was cleared within an hour. Post addresses were changed, bills redirected, boxes were piled high, and Dusty was riding shotgun beside me and my mate. My mother took her seat in my sister's car, strapped on her seat belt, and bid farewell to the life she hated. At that time, it was our belief that the history we shared with Tom was sealed when we shut the front door. The low sound of the heavy movement the lock made as it secured the door echoed inside the empty house. With very few objects softening the sounds, I fantasised over how Tom would react when arriving home to an empty shell, realising his subject had run away. We sped down the motorway and then, a few country lanes later, we were in the little village where my mother's hero was waiting for us. By this time the cold, wintery night had set in and the drone of rush hour traffic reverberated through the stark trees in the far distance. Box by box, we unpacked our rescued cargo into the safehouse. Within no time at all, a tidy pile of boxes lined the living room of the until then bachelor pad. She took her time slowly unpacking the contents of the cargo, and the dog happily played in the garden.

I hugged my mum tightly, and for the first time in months, I felt real warmth and compassion from her. She uttered a tearful thank you then released me and preceded to hug and thank my friend too. I told her I loved her and was so happy that after all these struggles she could finally relax. I gave her another goodbye kiss, telling her I would see her when I came back from the Falklands, sometime before the spring. I called over my energetic dog, and hugged him tight too, scratching his furry front legs up and down, a gesture he always returned with a loving head bump. I patted the good boy, assuring him I'll be back again soon. Perhaps, now with my mother settled, he would finally find his rightful place with my father who could look after him much better as he could walk and exercise the dog regularly, something she couldn't do. Lastly, I turned to the man who willingly accepted my troubled mother, firmly shook his hand and gently pulled him in towards my shoulder. Understanding that some contact between two men requires more than just a simple handshake, it was only right that I embrace him strongly.

Finally, I thought, she was safe. Now a page in her life was ready to turn and the final sentence of the chapter appeared as if a happy ending was approaching. My clouds of anxiety towards her situation started to evaporate and reveal deep, endless skies shining with the love of a million stars, just like holes in the floor of heaven. The compassion that everyone involved was feeling made our hearts come alive. With so much love present in that living room, the anguish of so many people in different ways was finally put to a definitive end, but the words and actions of the next twelve hours would be enough to unpick me from my seams, and let loose the tempestuous seas of the mental turmoil surrounding my marooned sanity.

***

My friend and I returned the borrowed van and started on our way back to Lincolnshire, one hundred and fifty miles away. I had a few days leave before my deployment to the Falklands would begin, so I packed the long list of things I needed for the months I'd be away into two large black military holdalls and placed them in my car. One last look around my small room and I flicked off the light. Bandit's stuff was packed in the car too, and we had just enough time for one little night time walk before I picked up his long fuzzy body and popped him on my shoulder while we wandered back to the car. I gave him a blob of WD-Ferrety (an oil-based ferret treat) on his tummy and placed him on the hammock in his cage. He sat like a big lazy bear while licking the treat he craved off from his little belly. I started the engine and drove the short distance off the airbase to the rescue centre I adopted him from.

I was about to leave Bandit behind and travel eight thousand miles away from the UK to a place better suited for penguins than ferrets, but I knew that he would be looked after there by his so-called grandparents until I returned home. I gave my little buddy a scratch underneath his spike studded leather collar, a kiss on the head and wished him farewell. Bandit didn't seem to get on too well with other boy ferrets, so he was placed in a cage with the ladies. As you can imagine, there wasn't an upsetting moment of farewell from Bandit. As soon as his paws touched the ground, he was surrounded by a dozen single ladies all eager to sniff and introduce themselves to the new bachelor on the scene. I didn't worry once about Bandit while I was away from him in his lovely little ferret hotel, as I know I certainly wouldn't have had anything to worry about if I had been locked away in a hotel for four months with a dozen single women either! I started back south again, the journey would take me three hours and I would arrive at my adopted family and that comfortable sofa just after midnight.

The following morning I arose early from my sofa. A weak November sun shone through the window, melting away the frost of that previous night and illuminating a thousand dewy droplets sparkling like jewels in the abandoned webs the spiders had left behind. For the first time, I realised that every waking moment of my life since joining the RAF had been plagued with an uneasy feeling for my mother's comfortability and vulnerability. But this morning, a calm easiness seemed to wander through the silence of my un-fogged, liberated mind. The peace I was experiencing was from the reassurance that she was now safe in the hands of a new carer, far away from the man of so many of her dramas. I calmly slipped on my clothes, folded the bedding away that had been used to cover the sofa so many times before, put on my shoes and stood outside in the liquid sunlight of that cold morning. Though the rays coming through the leafless branches were reluctant to impart the same heat as they had done in the summer, I was warmed by the comforting feeling of nature, love and after so many months of insecurity, peace. There, beneath that tree on the sloping front drive, I again found a deeper connection with myself, far away from my boisterous behaviour with airman friends and egotistical pursuits that hid away my true nature. Oneness seemed to oose from every nook and cranny of my spirit as I closed my eyes and assessed the damage, heartache, love and growth from the chapters of my life that I had overcome, ultimately ending with my mother's rescue. Every lesson I had to learn filled my heart while I stood there in silent appreciation of life and the unfolding universe around me. I connected again to the memories of my inspiring realisations outside the church on the hill three years ago. A swirling pattern of cause and effect shifted left and right in my head as I smiled through all the thoughts and memories of how spite led me to find belief in my own strength, homelessness led me to find a wonderful family and how I discovered through the toughest of nights, it's is always darkest just before the dawn. I stood in silent meditation, appreciating the wonders of my small existence, when from within my pocket there came an unsettling *bzzz-bzzz-bzzz*.

I rarely received phone calls as most people at the time knew how I often worked irregular hours and would arrange a time to call first by text, but even then, it was 0730 on a Saturday morning! What kind of mad person calls at 0730 and expects their call to be answered?! I took out my phone and found it was my sister calling. She had stayed in Essex with my wonderful Grandma the night after our 'rescue operation'. We had arranged the previous day to meet up in the morning so all of us could go and have breakfast together. I suspected this call was to clarify where and when we were meeting, But 0730?! What was she thinking! I took the call, answering cheerfully, though I felt a pang of uneasy speculation in the back of my mind. Perhaps my surprise meditation that morning served as a precursor to assure me that while everything had a purpose, things weren't going to get easier, in fact, they would get much harder. "I have some bad news about

138

Mum," she said hesitantly, "last night, after we dropped her off, Tom called her and demanded an explanation. She told him where she was, and he took her back home with him." A wave of sickness pulsed through my body, but she had more to tell me;

"She told him that *you* forced her to leave."

Lessons from Obligation and Love

"Even after all this time the sun never says to the earth, 'You owe me.' Look what happens with a love like that. It lights the whole sky." – Hafiz

Unconditional Love

It is often taught that us mere humans cannot love unconditionally; however, I believe unconditional love is a special, rare thing that is partly innate ability and life experience. Some may instantly begin to argue of the ability to love something unconditionally is easy, it is what they do with their wives or children and its love they have previously experienced as a young person, like when their grandmother loves and cherishes them. But when such an argument is challenged with the idea of your wife or husband having a long term affair, becoming abusive towards you or other family members or betraying the trust of someone irreparably, the vail of unconditional love that has been dressed over the relationship often falls. That, of course, is not unconditional love, but a love that will be present *so long as* certain conditions are met.

The unconditional love that western people most strongly connect with is that of God and Jesus Christ. My struggle with God's unconditional love is that he will love me forever, regardless of who I am and what I do, and there will always be a place in heaven for me… *so long as* I love him back just as much and glorify his name, else eternal damnation is yours for the keeping. Again, a condition to his apparent unending love has to be met. The difficulty with loving unconditionally is so very tricky to find in its purest form, that even God has struggled with it! I do believe unconditional love is achievable in small steps and can be developed further and further towards not some archaic, superhuman sense of unconditional love, but a well-formed understanding of plain old, ordinary love experience in a truly wholesome way.

I walked into a large Homebase store one afternoon while on a lunch break. I was browsing for items to put into my bathroom, and once I had trekked up and down the many isles, getting lost amongst dusty shelves of DIY supplies, I found the items I needed. I walked back through the labyrinth of enormous orange shelving and worked my way to the till. At the checkout, I noticed a small, unhealthy looking plant. On the terracotta pot, a number of labels had been placed over one another, firstly reading £4.50, then a big reduced sticker at £2.50, then another at £1.50, then finally, another reduced sticker was selling the unhappy plant at just 50p. It was a small money plant, the same kind my mother had owned and looked after in all the years of my life that I remember, so I felt some affinity with it. I picked it up, observed its damaged, yellowing leaves, split branches and dry soil, and decided to rescue this new friend from almost certain death on a forgotten shelf next to the other items that had been damaged in their life in the store. Once I was home, I set about to fix its injured branches, remove its yellowing, dead leaves and most importantly leave it in my sink overnight to absorb all the moisture it could. By the end of the first few days in my care, the plant had started to become healthy once again. The plant was only small, and it required very minimum attention, but I diligently took time every day to glance over at its place on my window shelf to examine its healthy existence.

The reason I've included an in-depth study of my little money plant is because plants are fantastic individuals to practise unconditional love with. I had an affectionate urge to look after that plant and developed a kind of love towards it, the word love being used in a liberal sense of the term. While I don't love my family the same way I love the plant, it still encompasses the four letters needed to express deep respect and admiration for something. At no point did I ever think to myself, "yeah, I like the plant, but I'd like it more if it grew faster." I never had feelings of judgement towards how it chose to grow, how it didn't look the same as a healthy money plant at first, or how it drained time away from other activities in my life. Of course I didn't, it's a plant! People don't go around judging plants! And that is exactly why looking after a plant is such a fantastic method to develop an understanding of what it means to love something regardless of its health, appearance, history or the time and space it takes up in your life. So, if caring for a plant is so easy and a wholly non-judgemental activity, why do we struggle to love fellow human beings the same way? They are much friendlier than plants, much more attractive in some respects, can return the love you give and are undoubtedly perfect in whichever way they are.

When I walk in the woods, I see all the twisted, randomised beauty of a thousand trees. Some are skinny and struggle in the absence of light,

142

while others are old and gnarled, with branches splintered and sagging. Some trees fall over and yet continue to grow to their environment, clinging to life by just a few roots, whereas others are planted firmly and almost encapsulate the characteristics of the 'perfect' tree, such as what a child might draw in a picture. Though all the trees are different, we never say this tree is too small, too big, too twisted or even too woody! We love and admire the woods for exactly how they are. Their imperfection and randomisation of their planting, growth and difference in appearance are what makes a wildwood beautiful.

So just like the trees in the woods, humans can be tall, short, fat or skinny. They can look tidy and clean, or rough and dirty. They can also be cruel, but more commonly they can be kind. Our place individually isn't to judge another person, but to accept that who they are is a direct reflection of their environment, upbringing and what they accept as their reality. When it comes to loving someone that you have some kind of relationship with, I always imagine my love for them in a metaphorical sense. Imagine your love represented as your hand and the butterfly is the person you love. When you hold a butterfly, you gently wrap your fingers around its shape, but you only allow its legs on the palm of your hand to be the only thing touching you. You mustn't hold it so tight that your fingers touch its wings, or even tighter so that you squish it. In your loose, softly closed hand, you can enjoy holding, feeling and observing the butterfly, enjoying the experience seeing one of the most beautiful of all nature's creations. When the butterfly wants to leave, your hand is loose and open enough so that all you need to do is slightly move your fingers and its gone, on its way to visit flowers and do butterfly things. So to must you hold the love of another gently, and when that other person spreads its wings towards the direction of a new career, new love or any other potentiality that most people would judge as selfish or heartless, just let them go, and have an unconditional trusting that the person's purpose here on Earth is going to be met one way or another, partly owing to the fact you allowed them to leave.

In the act of this unconditional allowing, you too will find your love better off knowing it has operated unjudgmentally, without being owed anything and without a feeling of a love lost, just a love experienced and cherished for exactly the creative, constructive wonder that love is. Imagine how many artists have been stifled by the love of parents wishing their children to become lawyers instead of artists, how many musicians were silenced by a teachers longing for them to seek a degree in physics or geniuses longing to work in medical research, instead sent to work in the family business rather than discover a cure for cancer.

Companionship

In order to align yourself with harmonious experiences and ultimately inner peace, you cannot do it alone. At some point, companionship must be struck between you and someone or something else. While companionship is often experienced through friends and lovers, it is not strictly limited to these people alone. Bandit and I certainly had a strong companionship, and we most certainly were friends, but I believe there is a much larger difference between companionship and friends that should be explored here.

The most common definition of companionship is 'a feeling of fellowship or friendship'. It is 'a feeling of' friendship', but not '*the* feeling of friendship'. I like to think of companionship as a term given to someone or something sharing a common goal, agenda or destination with you. A companion can be an individual you meet on a long train journey, holiday or on a non physical endeavour such as a group of start-up directors, discovering you share common ideas, though not always the same, and strike up a shared relationship with its foundation firmly rooted in a temporary common ground. This doesn't mean they will become your friend outside this common ground, but it does mean that, while you're engaged on that journey, your temporary friendship can be as influential as that with a life long friend, though it will only last until the journey is over. After the journey, you may find that companion a friend, though many times companions only last as long as your adventure. The concept of animal companionship or even companionship with things or feelings is just as powerful. Bandit and I had a strong friendship which grew from years of companionship shared through many journeys and adventures. I began to understand through his expression, pace or attitude what it was that he needed, such as a break, food, to walk an easier path or to have water. Giving him exactly what he needed allowed me to have a better understanding that truly, I was not alone.

That loving fulfilment towards another entity other than yourself, not because you are friends, but because you are sharing a similar journey, adventure or experience in life is true companionship. The same feeling of companionship can be seen between me and my walking boots, which the same pair have travelled the world with me. They've kept my feet warm in the South Atlantic, dry in Northumbria and secured my ankle tightly across rocky Mediterranean trails. Though the boots can never return any feelings of compassion, companionship edges towards not just a mutual understanding of two separate entities, but a paradoxical individual sense of togetherness between two things. Without those boots, I may have had more uncomfortable experiences, colder, wetter feet or even perhaps a twisted ankle. The feeling of gratitude is the strongest characteristic of companionship.

The common ground between my mother, her gardener, my sister and the man who took her in was found between us all, even though I had only met the gardener and the man she was to live with just a handful of times. The emotional test we found ourselves wrapped up in while trying to rescue her from Tom was a journey, one we all shared at the same level as each one of us cared immensely for her. My sister, mother and I found an even deeper companionship, as our journey following her illness and realisation of the cruelness of the man she was living with was a journey we had all been on for a much longer time. Often, the only difference between a stranger and a companion is immense gratitude for meeting a commonly aligned person, instead of facing them with triviality as we do with most people that we meet in our lives. So wholeheartedly welcome all people, pets or things in your life that travel with you on different journeys, whatever these journeys are. Become infinitely grateful for their companionship and you will find your reward is incredible fulfilment because of their part in your world.

Hope

Hope is a subject that can be easily misunderstood. In the situations I found myself experiencing, I required large amounts of hope to keep myself motivated and secure in the knowledge that one day the great waves of mental health that lived below my thin layers would eventually ebb away. Hope that a better life was out there for me was a great instigator of courage to keep ploughing through threatening encounters when I lived with Tom. Hope became another great help for me as with it, I could start imagining my mother in better conditions. It was my hopeful imagination that allowed a plan to be formed that would eventually lead to our small group of companions to move her away from her troubled home life.

While hope can achieve great things for people experiencing difficulty, it can become an addictive and troublesome aid to switch off. Things in motion stay in motion, and hope is no exception. Using hope as motivation to remove yourself from a situation can become a habit you can slip into once you have achieved that which you have hoped for, but humans tend to always want more. Once you have the circumstances you have hoped for, you again will find yourself hoping for another idealistic situation and another and so on. When you find yourself caught up in this cycle, you never truly allow yourself to live in the very moment you are in, content and happy with what you have. How can you expect to be fulfilled and happy when you are always hoping that better times are coming but aren't here yet?

Working from the premise that you want to release yourself from initial suffering, hope can be an incredibly powerful tool in your inventory. Hope, as I like to think about it from Wayne Dyer's teaching, is deciding for yourself that no one knows enough to be a pessimist about anything. In a world with infinite possibilities and outcomes, who are any of us to be so disheartened that we can't hopefully imagine for ourselves the possibility of a situation being escaped, an objection overcome or a dream come true? Hope today for your better world and as soon as it arrives, live in the now, the only moment you can thoroughly enjoy.

Microscopes and Telescopes

"If a man knows not to which port he sails, no wind is favorable." – Seneca

We met at a café near my grandma's bungalow where my sister began to explain the devastating news to me. She had asked us to help her and not only remove her from the situation, but also all her belongings too. Five individuals, travelling hundreds of miles and hours of time to assist her, and at the first inevitable encounter with her 'old' life she had, she not only gave herself up but placed all the blame on her rescuers. In my personal experience, never has there been a greater betrayal than what she did in the hours following us helping her. That fateful morning had started with such vivid feelings of tranquillity, but just moments later a confused, broken daze encompassed my being. I recognised in myself that I had done everything possible to preserve our relationship, relocate her to safety and end suffering for both her and I (and the rest of her family), but her inability to accept and embrace the love we all so freely gave to her was out of our control. I had no other choice than to accept her decision and come to terms with the fact that, because she had wrongly told Tom I was the mastermind behind this, Tom now wanted my blood more than ever. Her betrayal, after so much effort to save her and after so much love we all felt the day before, became the catalyst for my approaching appointment with a mental health emergency.

I still had a couple of days of leave before I was due to fly out of the UK, but the hours I had planned to enjoy in civilian freedom before months of military limitations were overshadowed by my heartbreak. How could a mother do that to her own son? Why, after everything we did for her, would she throw it back in our faces like that? I know he could be violent to others, especially me, but I began to wonder if she had also lied about Tom's abuse towards her. I sealed myself off from all feelings. A bewildered glaze subdued my mind while the stirring depression that I had masked under the role I played as the boisterous young military man swelled within me. I felt as if all I knew about love came from my early years of developing as a child. On one occasion when I was about 7, I remember wondering if I could marry her when I grew up because I knew marriage was for love, and I thought I could never love someone as much as her. It seemed natural to me that a mother never gives up on her child. Even as savage as nature can be, it is often recorded that mothers will stay with their dying, sick or stranded young until they themselves die of exhaustion protecting their child's life. Samantha had taught me that 'When we have children, part of our hearts exist on the outside of us.' How then could a woman who had just cried for help and depended on the loving protection of her family betray her son so easily to the man who she knew spent so much time making his life difficult?

The day before I was due to travel on the eighteen-hour flight to the South Atlantic, I sat alone feeling empty and confused. It had been days since I had felt any feelings other than mild, tainted appreciation for Samantha's loving care and sympathy for my distress. I quickly realised that while I was so hurt that emotional feeling had departed my consciousness, physical feelings hadn't left me. The experience of betrayal was a matter of the mind, but I quite quickly found a way to link my physical body and my cognition through self-harm. I longed again for feelings, just like a free diver longs for air, or how you thirst for cold water after hard work on a hot day. Without hesitation, I drew the small penknife blade that I carried with me across the patch of skin behind but between my index finger and my thumb. The instant relief gave me a rush of feeling that I craved, as if I had sliced through the ropes I found my soul entangled within. I found that self-harm was like finally sitting back in an armchair after a long day, so I set my head back, nestling myself into the Lazyboy of pain I had found myself enjoying, and cut into my hand once more, smiling through the pain, the only feeling I had felt in days. This would now be my coping mechanism for the entirety of my time at RAF Mount Pleasant, and as I fell deeper into despair, I relied on it further and further, cutting more, and deeper. The cutting was painful and I didn't enjoy the feeling of torn skin, but it was the overwhelming feeling of my brain processing the pain that was welcoming. The joy of the stimulation it gave me was worth the pain received from the blade.

***

A month into my deployment, and it was Christmas time (Christmas time has been dramatic a few times now in this story!) I was deployed at the same time as a friend from basic training, who noticed right away the cuts along my hand. I told her that it was from Bandit's scratchy claws. It had been weeks since I held Bandit, and she knew that too. She eyed me suspiciously, but compassionately. I put my hand out of sight and promised myself that I had to be more careful in the future. On the surface, I must have seemed like a happy, regular guy on a very mundane deployment to the Falkland Islands and that's how I wanted it to remain. I felt a coward for the confusion of states I was in and why I couldn't sense any emotion. I would do everything I could to distract myself from my lack of feelings. I trained hard at the gym during this time, often going two times a day, five times a week. I looked and felt the most physically fit I had ever been. I always looked after my uniform, dedicated myself to the work I had, though I didn't have much, and attended all the social events (getting drunk) that were available. On top of this, I still spent many hours alone observing the unique nature in the islands, seeing the historical sights and solo adventuring off-road over dunes, through rivers and onto beaches in the MOD Land Rovers. I gave no reason for anyone to suspect any suffering was being endured. But I had now started to cut myself on my upper inner arm, where it was unlikely to be spotted by the couple of concerned friends who now asked more intimate questions about how I was doing, all of which I laughed off, ashamed to open up.

I was a battlefield ambulance driver for the duration of my time there, a lonely position as I worked in a very small medical centre and would spend most of my days alone, waiting for any emergency calls. In the four months I was there, the call came in only five times, a grand total of one 'real job' every three weeks. While my mornings were spent preparing the fleet of ambulances, cleaning them and ensuring they were fit for purpose, my days were spent alone, in a small crew room with three tatty blue sofas, a large flatscreen TV with just one channel, British Forces Broadcasting Service, which played the same programs over and over again. I rented a plethora of books from the library, documentary DVDs and taught myself basic German. But these immensely boring twelve-hour, two days, two nights, two off-shift rotations were taxing to my already crippled mental health. While sometimes I felt I could put up levees in my mind to stop the waves of depression breaking them down, other times I was submerged in a desolate ocean of despair. I would tire of reading after a few hours, or become bored with TV which I used to distract myself from my condition, so I would roll up my sleeve and cut away at my already sore, swollen flesh. Like a shot of life through my veins, I would be able to settle and breathe deeply as my brain occupied itself with fighting the pain for a few moments, forgetting about its depression. An hour from then, and I would be swelling with misery once more and would be ready for another cut.

One sunny day, I recall sitting outside in the shelter of the small courtyard bordering my solitary crew room. The sun is a rare commodity in the Falkland Islands, and when it shows it only stays briefly. I was enjoying the warmth while sat on the dusty surface of a paving slab when a glittering in the pebbles bordering the perimeter of the courtyard caught my eye. I reached out to it and found a sharp shard of clear glass, no more than one-inch square. I felt its irregular razor edge with my thumb, rolled up my sleeve, and cut along my arm deeper than I had done any other time. While I wasn't sure if the wound may have been deeper because of the tool I used or if it was because my condition was worsening and I was pushing harder I did not know, but certainly the feeling of relief was blissful. I didn't like the blood, and often the cuts would get very sore which I didn't enjoy, but the initial separation of two sides of my skin gave me a wave of satisfaction as new feelings flooded from my body to my brain.

***

For a month now, the sensation of self-harm was the best and only feeling I experienced other than the beating I was putting myself through at the gym. I would box for an hour for training most nights at the latest possible time so as to avoid other people, but my last five minutes were usually spent on a heavy bag without gloves or wraps. I would always split my knuckles and leave blood dripping from my hands and smeared on the bag. Almost ceremoniously, I would clean the bag with the disinfectant spray provided for people to use on equipment after they had used it to train their bodies, not after they took out their mental health on heavy bags! Feeling totally out of control as my self-harm spiralled, it took more and more courage to keep up my regular, happy appearance. I welcomed in the new year of 2016 from inside the small space of the dark, cold and silent church at RAF Mount Pleasant, allowing thoughts of my past and my mother to flood back to me, rendering me in a mass of tears, hunched over on a pew at the back row. Drunken revellers noisily made their way past the large double doors, and I would wish they'd walk in, catch me off guard in a broken mess and talk me around to getting the help I so desperately needed. The confusion and vicious circle I had entered myself into from the weeks of self-harm I was inflicting backed me into a corner I felt I could not escape from. I thought about asking for help, but the chance of recovery seemed so remote, and the ease and accessibility of cutting myself appeared to me at the time to be the only way I would ever feel emotions and sensations ever again. I couldn't see how seeking medical and pastoral help would repair the damage I had allowed into my life from the culmination of my spirit being bent and broken so many times by the people I thought I could trust. Two

154

weeks from that point, I still had not checked myself into the doctor or confessed my issues to anyone, and by not 'checking in', I began to prepare for my suicide, or as I call it, my 'check out'.

One night in January 2016 I had just finished my night shifts and was ready for two days of downtime. A film about frontiersman Hugh Glass, who survived unbelievable odds while injured and abandoned two hundred miles from the nearest civilised encampment, was screening at the small cinema on the airbase. The film, starring Leonardo Decaprio, was titled 'The Revenant', and as an admirer of early American pioneers, I had been looking forward to seeing it for quite some time. I walked the enormous length of the cold corridor being blasted by the Antarctic wind to the cinema alone, purchased a ticket and took my seat by myself in the dark and almost empty screen. Early on in the film, an enormous bear attacks and maims the protagonist in a graphic, violent and incredibly realistic scene. True to the real tale, the man kills the bear but is left with several patches of flesh torn from his back, revealing his ribcage, a broken leg, slashed throat and countless other injuries. The next part of the film depicts DiCaprio's suffering as he's hauled over rough forested terrain. He is semi-conscious, cannot speak and is up against immeasurable pain, but the most rememberable of these sufferings that my attention focused on was the strained and painful sounds he made as he desperately clung to life.

It was in these scenes that I suddenly realised I was unable to move, and my eyes became fixed on the empty space between me and the screen. I was struggling to breathe and began gasping for air. Quickly, my attention switched from the movie to a film of my own, projected over what I was experiencing outside of me. I was immediately plunged back to my mother's bedroom the morning she had her stroke. I was reliving a scene from my past which was a perfect clone of what I had seen and heard so many years ago. Even the terror within that I was feeling was the same as I had endured before, as for a second time I watched her slip into the arms of disability through my flashback. The scene of my living nightmare then switched from her room to the various hospital wards she recovered in for months after the ordeal. Like a dream, I wasn't just witnessing the scene as if it was a TV screen, what I was experiencing was an all-encompassing internal affair that dragged my physicality and consciousness into the past. After four or five minutes in this depressive, painful bubble, clarity returned to me and I found myself back in the real world.

My focus gradually returned to the screen and the feeling of immovability disappeared soon after. My hands had cramped from being screwed up into tight fists for so long and the back of my t-shirt was wet from sweating profusely. My face too was wet from a stream of tears I couldn't hold back, they drenched my chin and neck. I watched the rest of the film quietly, concerned with what had just happened. It was so far removed from any experience I had had before and I began to doubt the event had happened as if it were a hallucination or drug-induced vision. I walked back to my accommodation, slumped on the faded blue armchair (exactly the same as the chairs in the crew room), took the piece of glass I had kept from my previous cutting at work and pressed it hard against my skin, injecting a spike of well-needed adrenaline to my brain. A few cuts later, and my despair had stilled enough so that I could begin to understand what had just happened. While the flashback in the cinema was clearly

156

replaying a tragic experience in my life, I felt my past wasn't awful enough to bring my mental health to such a place as to cause me to have flashbacks! Flashbacks, as far as I knew of them, were experiences some comrades had suffered from when returning from combat tours after witnessing the horrific reality of war, or even just from being on constant high guard to explosions, mortar and rocket attacks. Witnessing the illness of my mother and the subsequent feelings attributed to that rough time at home, depressing hospital visits and dreadful relationships didn't seem a good enough excuse to have *flashbacks*! I was confused and frustrated at my mental health. I felt ashamed for my selfishness, like a spoilt child thinking the world was against me, crying 'it's not fair!' But it was real. The mental episodes were agonising, and I wasn't attention seeking, in fact, it was my lack of seeking attention that had worn-down my health.

That next day, hollow from the previous event, I browsed the library for interesting biographical films and found one titled 'The Possibilities Are Endless', about the singer-songwriter Edwyn Collins, frontman of the indie band Orange Juice. Edwyn shot to global fame when he went solo, releasing the song 'A Girl Like You', featuring a catchy, electrically charged guitar riff that echoed across the planet. In 2005, Edwyn tragically suffered two strokes which completely rewrote his brain and physical ability. Like my mother, Edwyn lost much of his speech and the function of one side of his body. While the film is an incredible cinematic experience, complete with edgy camera work and haunting audio, it captures the embodiment of the courage and love that inevitably led to Edwyn's recovery and new album. Though it is a wholly uplifting piece of art, the first few minutes capture a healthy, energetic Edwyn playing his songs on a popular American TV show, but then the scene cuts to a black screen, with deep, unsettling bassy sounds and suppressed noises, like a haunted, submerged echo. Then, Edwyn's voice, distorted from the stroke, plucks at words and tries to string a sentence together, but what comes out is simply *erm - erm - aah - la a - nn - nnn - shes erhh - fuck - Wwwwwhats happening tttoo me?* The disturbing struggle he undergoes to speak his mind was exactly the same noises and process of thought my mother made as she gradually regained her cognition, but this was the first time I had heard it in many years, and the first I had experienced it while enduring an episode of poor mental health.

As if the DVD was a time machine, the words and sounds immediately locked up my body and sucked me back again into a world of painful emotions, instantly causing me to relive the many hours spent seeing her unconscious, Tom's oppression over me and all other hurtful circumstances I encountered at that time. The twisting visions and feelings ran through my mind chaotically for a much longer period this time, and when I came around to my senses, soaking wet from sweat and tears, the film was almost thirty minutes through. I came to realise that sound seemed to be the trigger that set off my newly acquainted flashbacks, just as the sound of DiCaprio's slashed throat as he groaned and stammered after his attack brought on a flashback at the cinema. This time, Edwyn's courageous rendition of his stroke and his recovery story had set off a ripple of mental gridlock that not only occupied my mind, but my body also. When I came back to my senses, I ripped at my arm once more and collapsed on my bed alone, eight thousand miles from Samantha, my family and Bandit. I was also thousands of miles away from the root of my problems back in England, but they would soon find me again in the following days.

***

Feeling totally defeated, I called upon my old basic training friends and explained exactly what I was experiencing. As I didn't have the courage to confide in a professional, they let me know that they would seek help for me. The next day at work I had a visit from an RAF Padre, a Presbyterian minister. He sat with me briefly and told me that my friends were concerned and that firstly, speaking to him was totally my decision, secondly, anything I should say to him would be handled extremely sensitively and would be totally confidential. He told me where his office was, attached to the church. Asking no more questions, he left me and bid me a good day.

A sudden rush of relief swept over me, and the weight of my situation lifted slightly as I discovered a problem shared is a problem halved. That same day I booked a twenty-minute slot to use the Skype computers in a very old and neglected internet access suite called 'Area 51'. I spoke to my sister about my self-harm, the recent flashback episodes and how that day I made the first step towards seeking help. Towards the end of the call, we discussed our mother, and how her condition was getting worse. While I knew that was the case, I didn't know that she had been taken to the hospital a few more times since I left the UK, as it was suspected that she may have had further strokes.

We ended the call, and I began to feel that in my decision not to speak to her any longer to preserve my sanity, I had opted to be a bystander while she slipped away from life. Apart from a short text message at Christmas, I hadn't spoken to her since I left the UK in November. Armed with the knowledge of myself I gave to the Padre, we had a clear, substantial topic to explore. It wasn't my mother. It wasn't Tom. It wasn't guilt over my mental health. It was merely my *reactions* to all these things, and my reaction to finding myself in this situation.

While talking to the Padre over a number of days, he convinced me to finally seek medical help. I had put off a meeting with the station medical officer because I knew that if I had any episodes of mental health issues on my record, I could kiss goodbye to the career in aviation I was seeking.

Unfortunately, in all services, mental health is still seen as a life long ailment and weakness, not as an injury that can be treated and exercised. If I had broken an arm or leg I would be given medical attention, taken off duty until my injury was repaired, and once I had the all-clear, I could carry on with my career and further pursue my ambition to become aircrew if I chose to. The military still does not recognise a mental injury in the same light as a physical injury or disease such as cancer. Though their symptoms are in different realms of the body, treatment, aftercare and check-ups should provide everything needed so that a person's career isn't scrutinised just because of a mental injury. The added pressure as a young male to seek help by a mental health professional carried a taboo with it, and while speaking with friends in the military who had similar episodes, they too felt like they couldn't approach a professional without jeopardising their aspirations or feeling weak amongst other men.

As I sat down with the medical officer, he asked me before he started his diagnostics, did I realise that I was putting my career on the line and that

160

once this is filed, you limit the potential to go further in your career? These comments were made off record, and I know he was simply being kind and letting me know the truth, but this archaic, old fashioned approach to mental health is further damaging our society and especially young people who are growing up being told and believing that being open and honest about their health is the best and right option to take, but in doing so they simultaneously limit their ability to grow and develop in a world that judges their future ability on even the smallest historical episode in their mental health – the most fragile area of human health. I am not experienced enough or medically trained to comment further on these matters, I just hope that in fifty years' time our institutions would have moved beyond these limiting ideas.

I divulged my hidden health to the medical officer, and once finished, returned to my quarters. Taking my note pad, a pen and the book I was reading, I walked down the never-ending corridor towards the haven of the small, volunteer-run café, Oasis. I ordered a banana bread cake (one of the few tasty delights found on the base) and took my seat. I read my book in calm silence, undistracted by the groups of personnel around the room in military and civilian clothing playing Jenga, Cards Against Humanity and Scrabble. After enjoying a few pages of my read, I calmly opened the notebook, took the lid off the pen and began tentatively writing my suicide note.

Feeling no solace from the medical help I was receiving (a few pamphlets, a sit down talk with a lovely civilian nurse with a cup of tea and a few website links telling me its okay to feel the way I did – as if that is enough to stop someone's suicide), I expressed in my note how impossible I felt it was to go on with the feelings I had inside. I was crippled by flashbacks that would occur most days at any given moment, I would only receive a couple of hours sleep a night as I had developed indescribable nightmares and the only salvation I had come close to finding was through self-harm in many different, ever-growing ways.

Through my conversations with the Padre, I realised that the Falklands wasn't a place to escape your worries at home, but a place that magnified the problems. According to him, it wasn't uncommon to have problems at home spiral out of control while on deployment. Many people feel that they can look at their problems with a telescope and feel removed from their home lives, when actually the abundant free time and ease of work made their minds focus on their issues, scrutinising them in minute detail, like a scientist with a microscope. While I had very little work to do, I filled my life with books, DVDs and learning, but there was only so many hours you can spend doing that day in day out for four months without your mind wandering.

Knowing that my mother was suffering immeasurably, and I, her only son wasn't strong enough to speak to her, I felt like the only way out was to end it all finally. My suicide note wasn't written with tears in my eyes, or with a heavy heart. While I told my family and friends that I loved them, it was a very frank, stark and obvious answer to a very real problem in my life. Self-harm made it easier for me to live, but it didn't give me the final solution I was looking for. While that final solution was indeed peace and harmony, I thought that could only be achieved from changing the

162

world outside of me, and that there was nothing I could grow within to stabilise myself. I made it clear that my very few possessions should be sold, and all my savings donated to the ferret shelter that looked after Bandit while I was away. I was totally unable to see that my departure from this life would mark for me the end of witnessing sunsets, summer love, the smell of rain, flocks of birds flying south for the winter through crisp autumnal air and the other plethora of wonders the planet gives us so freely every moment of every day when we choose to see them over our own individual problems in life.

I left the note in the case of my telephone should I suddenly decide to find the right opportunity to end my life. I intended at this point to kill myself, though without any high buildings to jump from, substances readily available to overdose on or trains to swiftly end my life, I fantasised about other opportunities I may have. I decided that a violent, horrific end wasn't what I wanted. I was escaping the terrors in my life, so a terrifying end was something that didn't make me feel good to think about, whereas the appeal of simply falling asleep and not waking up was much better. I considered hanging myself, but I knew the horror of my friends working at the medical centre having to deal with my body could have scarred them for life. The most effective way I considered, would be to feed a pipe through to the cab of my Land Rover ambulance from the exhaust, but the time taken to do that would have been too slow and I may have been caught, and my attempt failing – Plus I didn't know where to get a hose that long! I kept my plans secret and attended more sessions with the Padre. I was requested to visit my commanding officer, who told me conversations had been had with him regarding my mental health, and I was asked what I wanted him to do.

Feeling a huge sense of embarrassment with the way the topic was handled, I assured him I didn't need to be returned back to the UK. I was treated by him and other medical staff as a young boy, away from home for the first time and making up the severity of my condition so I could get an early flight back. I can't blame them for thinking of me that way, it is a method that can be dishonestly exploited in the military to escape deployments. I felt a failure for accepting help in the first place. We agreed that having a stiff upper lip would be the best option, and I was sent away, never to receive further help. I suffered in silence for another month, observing the comings and goings of the aircraft destined for long flights home, the extremely turbulent weather changing from sunny days to winter storms (even though it was summer in the Southern Hemisphere, it still snowed a lot at this latitude) in a matter of hours, and the up and down experiences of my health between comfortable numbness, to imminent suicide.

Before my flight home, I grew a healthy understanding that by not talking to my mother as her health worsened, I made my life bearable, though painfully guilty knowing she may soon pass away. Not speaking to her tore me apart, but after the constant betrayals I was faced with from her and Tom, any further contact with her would have exposed me to more trauma, making it impossible for me to heal. Letting her into my life again and again had become too predictably distressing, the only way I found to avoid this was to close myself off from her. Through this understanding, the talks with my family (my sister especially) and Samantha, I eventually curbed my incessant self-harm and happily threw away the glass shard I had fallen in love with before I flew back to the UK.

Lessons from Microscopes and Telescopes

"A man with outward courage dares to die; a man with inner courage dares to live." - Lao Tzu

Flexibility

Throughout religious texts, historical manuscripts and today's modern world, water is a highly prioritised force. It goes without saying that water is the element that gives life to our planet and is the vital ingredient for life to exist anywhere in the cosmos. I find that water is a fantastic thing to study so we can begin understanding how our best course of life should be lived. Though water is soft and gentle, it is arguably the most destructive force on our planet, eroding land ceaselessly, destroying entire cities and even rising from apparently calm seas to form a tsunami of unstoppable power. However, a single drop of water is nourishing and a pleasant feeling on your face. We wash in it, enjoy sports in it and use it to sustain our lives. As water pours over a surface, it will flow until it meets resistance, then simply move around the object or pool until it rises above it. Once it has overcome its obstacle, the flow will carry on until that once gentle spring meets the entire ocean.

The flexibility of water reminds us that just because you can stay soft and gentle, it doesn't mean you are weak. Flexibility serves you as an enabler that allows you to flow easily to overcome complications or become hard and unwavering when faced with much harder circumstances that require more purposeful action. The potential of a single drop of soft, gentle water has locked inside of it the boundless depths of the entire ocean.

While trees are incredibly strong and enormously heavy, it's only owed to their flexibility that they are still here. When storms grab at their leafy boughs they twist and sway. Their trunks bend and shake with the winds, and sometimes even the roots can be seen lifting as they slacken and tense systematically through their anchoring effect. After the storm, the tree that looked so weak and pitiful against a hurricane remains standing tall, surviving due to its flexibility that seems incomprehensible on a calm day. Even then, when a tree is damaged in a storm, the flexibility of life within the tree heals the wound and it carries on living. On many occasions, I have seen trees in the woods toppled, its roots exposed to the sky, and yet new branches spring towards the sun as they grow upwards from the now horizontal trunk.

While finding the words to write this chapter, I was asked if I wanted to go for lunch with my partner's family. I was getting on well with my writing and didn't want to be disturbed, but I was begged and pleaded with, so I reluctantly said I would go. I visited the house of a friend of theirs who I hadn't met. As soon as I arrived at the beautiful Italian home, I was greeted like a friend instantly. We shared stories and thoughts in broken English and Italian and ate truly wonderful food together. I totally forgot my sulky

166

behaviour and became so grateful for the afternoon I was having. My refusal to be flexible at first made me feel uncomfortable as I was disturbed from writing, but once I allowed myself to enjoy the flow of life, I was inspired by the occasions that afternoon to write passionately about ideas that came to me during the day. Had I not been flexible, inspirations may not have come my way and my task at hand may have been a struggle to complete.

Have flexibility as one of your values and enjoy the process of bending and shifting your life to your circumstances. Resisting the storms of your life may snap your branches and rip you up from your roots. Sway with the coming and going of life, embrace the storms and sudden turns. Never be unmovable enough to allow damage to come your way and allow your pride to flex towards humility for yourself and all others.

Calm

In some moments I felt that if I could find a quick method to take my life right there and then, I would have taken it. Only through calmness did I find that I began to rationalise my feelings and chose to decide to bide my time and find a different occasion to take my life. Though this calmness was still urging me to take my life in a different way, it still bought me enough time where my attitude towards suicide would settle. Without that calmness and decision that I would find what I thought of as a less destructive way to 'check out', I may have irrationally (more irrationally than the irrationality of suicide to begin with) decided to slit my wrists, hang or electrocute myself.

Calmness in the face of overwhelming struggle is a virtue so important and should be employed every day to every situation you may face. Often when arguments arise or I'm met with stony-faced resistance, I remove my thoughts from the conflict and place my attention only on what I want to attract and feel in my life. If the argument is around me but I am not part of it, I close myself off to it, refusing to let my attention wander into the tumultuous waters of a fray, then pick up my book, and find another room to read it in. Mobile phones are a great method too for removing yourself from the situation, but remember to ensure you find any way to step back from a dispute, otherwise you may find yourself being encouraged to join in support of one side or the other.

Calm isn't only a feeling, but a tool that you can use to your advantage to remain focused in whichever kind of moment you wish to live in. While it can be relied upon to avoid an argument that you know will sort itself out in its own time without your assistance, calm can also be used when you find yourself in dire circumstances such as car accidents, becoming lost in the outdoors or while finding a solution to a financial problem. When you practice keeping a calm attitude enough times when in situations that may stir anxiety, you will become able to weather any storm. You wouldn't expect your pilot to panic on a routine flight to a holiday destination, though many times in an average flight, pilots are met with challenges to overcome, unexpected air traffic control commands to be adhered to and ever-changing weather conditions. When facing survival situations in the wilderness, say your typical desert island scenario, calmness of mind and rational thinking are the critical first steps experts insist must be embraced before forming a plan to figure out what you're going to do next.

168

Calmness of the mind is therefore critical, in not just securing peace and harmony, but also surviving any of life's challenging surprises.

Become the pilot-in-command of your own inner calm, practice resting on calm in a tricky circumstance and allow the slowing effect calmness has to quiet your mind and find a solution. Rationalising your thoughts while having your focus on the heavy challenge you face cannot bring you to the mental state of mind you need to operate from to achieve a solution to your problems. You cannot expect to escape from your problems by approaching them with the same mental attitude that got you into them in the first place. Nurture calm in your life always, and rational thinking will be your gift.

Occupy Yourself

One weekend prior to the start of my service, I visited my grandma and grandad. I was welcomed in by my grandma and once I had given her a hug, I asked where my grandad was. It wasn't unusual to not see him right away, he was often squirrelled away in his woodworking shed, making all manner of delightful wooden toys, scaled-down churches or miniatures of shops he remembers as a child. I made my way to the shed in the garden, but today I found him in the conservatory covered in white paint. He had a motorbike helmet in one hand, and a paintbrush in the other, applying layers of white paint to the helmet. I asked him what on Earth he was doing. He put down the helmet, reached into a box behind him and pulled out a white pair of painters overalls which he had stuck NASA logos and insignia to.

"I'm making an astronaut costume!" My eighty-year-old grandad was wonderfully eccentric with his occupations and surprising pass times, and clearly, today was no exception!

On countless occasions, I've heard mid-twenty-year olds start to discuss their pension plans, and how they are already looking forward to retirement. How many sixty-and-seventy-year olds reach their retirement and decide that they will now spend their lives doing *nothing*? Like the old lady seen every day at the bingo hall, or the old man in the same seat at the pub, these individuals have handed over their existence to time, waiting in their final years for their hearts to finally give out. If you are still here, you still have a purpose, and that purpose is to be fulfilled and ultimately serve others. Whether it's to make spaceman costumes, knit scarves for small craft fairs or start a new career in music, acting or painting, occupying yourself is vital to living the purpose of your life.

Occupy yourself with a passion or hobby. If you don't have one, start to look at the things you do enjoy. Discover for yourself what it is about that topic that you enjoy and find a way to engage with it more thoroughly. Ask how you can be in the service of others, improving their lives by sharing your passion with them. Give your time freely to helping others on their path by volunteering, helping at a youth club or supporting a local hospice in their kitchen once a week. Occupy your mind and when you delve into your old age, let the grim reaper know you're too busy enjoying the world to stop and simply do nothing!

Not only should our free time be full of inspiring occupations, but so too our livelihoods should be so enjoyable that the idea of retirement won't excite you at all. Dr. Shigeaki Hinohara, a Japanese medical doctor who studied longevity, claims that retirement has a detrimental effect on our brains and life span. He eventually past away at age 105, and until he died, he sometimes worked eighteen hours a day looking after patients, as that was the passion he lived for. Before his death, he advised that the secret to a long life is to never retire.

Read, learn and imagine! Venture into every day with a goal and work towards materialising a dream. At the very least, occupy yourself with a hobby or fulfilling service to others. Your time is truly the best gift that can be given, spending it in worthy occupations is the best investment you can make in yourself.

Life and Death

'Forgiveness is the fragrance the violet sheds on the heel that has crushed it.' – Mark Twain

I reached the UK in March 2016. After many weeks away from the UK I was much more broken than I had been before I left, suffering not just from a dreadful depression and self-harm, but also from the sickening feeling of having to break contact with my very unwell mother. I would wake up every night screaming fearfully, clutching to the sheets around me as my nightmares intensified. Sometimes flashbacks would strike me, though they had started to subside by this time. Worst of all were the panic attacks, one of which I remember hitting me as I queued up in a shop to buy raspberry doughnuts (my favourite!)

For those of you that haven't experienced a panic attack, imagine your vision suddenly zooms in intensely like a spotlight on only the things in front of you. Your body tenses and your heartbeat races so fast, forming a lump in your throat as it begs to be released from your body. Your hearing becomes so intense that every sound makes you jumpy, and the walls around you seem to loom and close in. Then, the overwhelming feeling of *'run!'* seems to scream from within you, and it becomes almost impossible to ignore. No matter where you are, what time it is or who you are with,

172

everything suddenly appears wrong, out of place and crooked. Recognising the event, I would have to stop what I was doing and find a space outside with very few people or movement and breathe steadily until the feeling disappeared. These events would last from two to ten minutes, a few times a week, but I never discovered what seemed to trigger them. My tendency to self-harm had diminished too, though I still had the intention set at the back of my mind that I would 'check out' when I found the opportunity, and therefore kept my suicide note, occasionally adding or subtracting from it.

During this time I was dating a really understanding and caring girl from my home town. She approached my suffering carefully and with great care so as not to judge or even ask what I was experiencing. Just in the same way Samantha gave me free, unfailing love, she too gave so much care for me in the times I would wake up in fits of hysteria, or help me to get away from situations quickly whenever I found myself entering into the arms of a panic attack. Though she never probed too deeply into my past, she did help me unravel the knotted history I had buried in my head and heart that ultimately led me to contemplate suicide. We were in contact with each other not too long before the day my sister and I rescued my mother, so she understood the difficulties I was experiencing while the sting of my betrayal rattled around in my head. She helped me in this time to realise that, now the dust had settled, the only way to establish why my mother had done the cruel things she did was to act with courage, meet her face to face and finally put the past to rest.

For the first time in months, I sent her a message letting her know I was back in the UK, and it would be nice if we could meet somewhere.

Knowing she adored Costa coffee, we arranged that we could meet in the high street of Southend. It was like every other April day before it, and a grey blanket of cloud above smothered the countless shopaholics as they spent their small salaries eagerly in the dozens of clothes shops littering the pedestrianised areas.

I arrived half an hour before we were expected to meet, making sure Tom didn't decide to lurk somewhere before our meeting. I was concerned that she would have told him of our arrangement and taken the opportunity to engage me in an argument or fight. I sat on a bench fifty meters from the coffee shop, anxiously keeping my eyes fixed on the faces that walked towards me. After the months of suicidal thoughts, a fight or further rapture wouldn't have served me well at all. My heart was pounding hard but steady. My hood was up and I may have looked a little out of place and timid, but my fists were clenched as I expected to defend myself from Tom if he appeared. By this point, she was five minutes overdue. I was certain that she had stood me up and wasn't going to show.

Through the small walkway between the cinema and the strip of retail buildings, the steady crowd of consumers were parted as they manoeuvred either side of a hunched over woman, walking very slowly and clumsily with a walking stick, taking one foot forward quickly and dragging the other behind her until it met her other foot again. She walked slowly and held up even elderly people as she staggered. Some people cut around her quickly and she lifted her drawn-out, sagging face towards them and muttered an inaudible insult at them, pointing at them with her stick like a grumpy old Mrs. Twit from Roald Dahl's famous books. Her right arm

174

swayed lifelessly by her side, and her hand formed a skinny, veiny claw. She pulled her tangled hair away from her face with her good hand, still clutching the cane, and walked shakily towards the coffee shop. It was inconceivable to believe that this unhealthy, crippled figure was the tyrant who's mere words I had allowed to push me to the point of cutting myself and contemplating suicide. Instantly, a wave of sympathy burst out from within as I sat watching her struggle to walk. Seeing her suffering, I disconnected from the pain she had caused me and immediately surrendered to loving compassion as my realisation of her condition set in. She took her seat slowly, looked around expectantly and took out her phone. Feeling a little silly that I would be so saddened at this frail woman, I took my hood down and walked the short distance to the table she had chosen.

We embraced each other while she was still sat down, as getting up was so much of a struggle for her. The hug seemed to last an eternity, and with all my judgements washed away, I connected with her in that moment stronger than at any point of our times together before. She had her hand around my neck, and I had buried my face into her shoulder, pressing my head hard against her. It was a feeling of immense displeasure to be in her company, but euphoric to be held so passionately by my own, biological mother. She tried to scramble for words and only managed a few broken *iii – oh – youuuu – ahhh – Iii – I'vvveee – ugh* sounds, but her lopsided smile and bright eyes gave away more of what she wanted to say than any of her words could. When excited or upset, she would struggle to form sentences well, but after we had both calmed ourselves and I had bought us both a coffee, I could just about understand what she was saying. We spoke about the Falklands, Christmas, our dog Dusty, her health and eventually why she had returned to Tom and why she had told him the lie that I forced her to move. She became very quiet and upset but kept listening, so I kept talking. I asked her why she didn't do or say anything during mine and Tom's fight on the grass, why she hadn't spoken up in my support during the argument with my sister and questions to lots of other events I haven't included in this book. She gave me no answers, only looked uncomfortable and upset. She interrupted me halfway through my questioning and told me exactly why Tom had left each time and why he often stayed away from home for days without reason. During the first few months of her hospital stay and much of the time since her return, Tom had been seeing another woman. He had been visiting this woman regularly while staying in a relationship still with my mother and living in their house with me, even while she was in hospital. He was refusing to take her swimming with him as he had been taking another woman out in replacement of her.

My heart broke into a thousand pieces at the realisation my intuition from the previous years had served me well, but at a painful cost. For months I had become a stranger to her, and the whole time, she too had become a stranger to herself and everyone she knew. She had pushed all her family and friends away as far as she could. I showed her my arm, where the scars from the cuts I gave myself still resided, and let her know that because of how she acted against her family, she damaged the lives of people around her who had once trusted and loved her so dearly. I told her that how she used me in the months after her divorce from my father, coupled with Tom's violent attitude, the way she had betrayed me after helping and believing in her so much and many other events had triggered an awful depression inside of me. Now knowing that this whole time she knew he was spending time with another woman, I couldn't bring myself to help her anymore, even after seeing how fragile and damaged she was. I told her how dearly I loved her, but that I couldn't help her again the way she wanted me to and needed me to in order to live out what life she had left in peace. I couldn't risk damaging myself any further, knowing how close I was to suicide, and how I still carried a suicide note just in case an event would put me back into that dark corner of my mind again.

Our coffees were half-drunk and cold, we had been speaking for over an hour. I decided our conversation had served its purpose and wanted to gradually wrap up my thoughts. Suddenly, as if I had just served her a great insult, her sad, regretful tone and appearance switched to a fit of nasty anger. She frowned heavily, put her head on a slight tilt and leaned in towards me. She began telling me how much of an awful son I was and explained, unjustifiably, that ever since I was a little boy she thought I was horrible. Pointing a bony finger at me she told me I deserved everything I had got, she was glad I was so unhappy. The speed and intensity in which her tone changed were so similar to when she had realised I was no longer under her control during the divorce, and her mind games and lies were no longer being tolerated by me. Sensing she had completely lost her mind, I told her I was listening, but that her words were falling far short of the pain she wanted to cause in me. She brought herself to her feet shakily, lit a cigarette and smoked it as she started a slow, fumbling walk to the taxi rank. After hailing a driver, she disappeared down the road, out of sight of my two cup coffee table, surrounded by pity and depression – but it wasn't my own. This time, the dark feelings experienced were that of a person pushed to desperation by the inability to cope with the physically limiting challenges that her health had bestowed upon her. Her conceited pride had disabled her from accepting the help of others and humbly accepting the limitation of her condition.

I had faced my demon, and finally put to rest some of the maddening thoughts that had consumed me. Through our conversation, years of unanswered questions had been resolved. After five years of struggle, my intuition was rewarded with the knowledge that I had been on the right side of the fence the whole time. Other than knowing and believing in myself that I was being used as a scapegoat and pawn in a much larger game, I had heard from the perpetrator of my suffering herself that I had been right all along, but this understanding didn't bring with it a sense of liberation or freedom from my past. While I was happy that I had settled years of lies in one conversation, I felt like a man wrongly imprisoned, released only after a stressful trial which could have been avoided if the evidence that trapped me so long was exposed in the first instance. The worse part of this bitter triumph was the fact that still my mother was sick, and had become further mentally unwell. No matter how many people tried to help her, or how they helped her (even a gentleman as far away as Israel would Skype her during state of the art medical therapy sessions), she had now walked herself down a one-way street that no one else was welcomed to walk with her. Knowing how she only wished to be left alone and made it clear how awful she thought I was, I knew I couldn't bring myself to re-establish a relationship again and I would have to leave it as it was. Though our conversation had given me a fighting chance at gradually recovering from my nightmares, panic attacks, flashbacks and suicidal thoughts, I knew my ultimate goal at having a caring biological mother again was unreachable.

178

***

I drove back to Lincolnshire that afternoon and finally reunited myself with The Bandit. I called into the cage he was sharing with a dozen or so lady ferrets. A mass of ferrets were bundled up together on some blankets, and though you could clearly see different colours and sizes, not a single individual could be made out from the pile of long skinny bodies, floppy arms, legs and goofy looking noses. I called his name, and the stockpile of weasels wiggled as their curious faces sprung up to see who was disturbing them. The familiar naughty face of my buddy Bandit popped up from the middle in a loved-up haze. I picked the little guy up for the first time in months and the women ferrets rushed to say goodbye to him at the mesh of their cage. It was wonderful being with him again and my heart elevated to the vibration of his lovely little chuckling sounds, but after so much time getting up to all sorts of mischief with his fanciers, he stunk! I told him to say goodbye to his girlfriends and warned him to remember, for next time, if he can't be good, he needs to be safe! We got home and I gave him a bath right away, the water turned yellow, so after one more soak, he was ready to dry off, chase a ball around for a while then fall asleep back in his own little cage, a bachelor once more.

Months flew by, and spring became summer, and summer through to late October. My responsibilities in the RAF ramped up considerably. I was now leading a handful of historical tours across the UK and abroad (which involved more pubs than museums) and I had trained and become a Bushcraft Instructor as a secondary duty. While the benefits of military life were clear, the actual benefits of life within the confines of the military were impossible to see. While the 'good stuff' included good pay, lots of holiday, unique experiences, and the ability for an enlisted airman to drag his or her feet until retirement age and not get fired, the bad stuff was much more present. We had a saying that we used often and can be applied to any area of life which was 'bullshit baffles brains'. This point is easiest explained during an inspection, where the turn out of your highly polished shoes and smart uniform just might allow your instructors to over look your awfully presented locker, thus your 'bullshit', has just baffled their 'brains'. But it appeared that the same rule applied the other way round too. Exercises in paperwork bullshit, formality bullshit and disciplinary bullshit for not wearing non-issue black socks was enough to baffle my brains.

In 1916, then Bishop of Ripon, Edward Arthur Burroughs wrote that the life of a military man was "Months of boredom punctuated by moments of terror." While this alludes to the horrors of the western front, my only experience of 'moments of terror' was being told we had an inspection the morning after a heavy night at the Black Swan pub. Other terrifying moments were being caught without a beret on by the SWO, not saluting a pompous just-out-of-Cranwell officer who was forty meters away (yes, I really was asked by an officer why I didn't salute her when she was so far away) and that moment of terror that out shadowed even nuclear war itself – being told your working the weekend! After four months sat in a dreary crew room, waiting for the emergency phone to ring, I had seen countless political debates and houses of commons speeches that looked to divide our countries military, sell of its vital organs to private companies, and lower the pay of personnel in the process. It seemed as if the government's problem with their expenditure, or lack of it, wasn't due to countless expensive conflicts and lack of ability to distribute government funding, oh no, it was Private Jones and his extortionate £18,000 a year salary. I had fallen out of love not with the job but rather fell out with the fact that young men and women were giving their lives to a country that didn't provide a fair service to them during or after their dedication. The narcissistic machine that consumes men and women's lives for a government's will was flawed, and I was unwilling to be a cog, no matter how small, in such a gross endeavour to bring around a peaceful world by bombing the life out of it.

This was solely my experience and that of some of my close comrades, though I do acknowledge and heartily thank and support the courage and diligence of individual soldiers, sailors and airmen on operations all around the world. Their struggle is real, and their individual bravery far from home, with their life outside of their control, are all true and enduring heroes of mine. It's their government that I condemn. But it's okay, because they stand at the cenotaph every November and feel very sad for the wars that have been fought, and vow never to do it again, only to return the next year when more names are added to the list of the honourable dead. I had voiced my concerns before with my superiors regarding my purpose within the military, and our militaries priorities concerning personnel, budgets and post-military life. I was urged to seek more involved positions and enrolled myself to the selection for aircrew, as was my initial plans way before joining. I studied hard, attended selection tests and visits to different stations and units, but rarely did I find a pilot or crewman entirely happy with their job and the state of the UK's military.

I walked into work one morning armed with a sense of disdain towards my career and announced to the dozen or so bored airmen sat in the crew room that I was resigning, and they could watch me sign away my fate. There was often personnel resigning over various issues, and watching them digitally end their career had become a form of sport. I took my game chair, settled the keyboard the way I like it, and turned on the PC. A crowd of hopeful airmen, still in their obligatory years where they are not permitted to resign, took out phones to video the event. I logged onto my personal administrative page on the MOD computers, typed in my details and clicked the career termination button, known as PVR (Premature Voluntary Release). I clicked yes to a list of questions similar to 'Are you sure you want to leave?', 'Are you sure you are sure?' and 'Do you not, not, not want to leave?' The die was cast, I clicked the final button, and my termination submission to my CO was sent through to his email inbox. My comrades cheered and wished me well, inspiring them that someday, they too can have their freedom!

Though the event was always taken light-heartedly, at the time the RAF had a serious issue with the number of leavers they were experiencing. Some trades were bribed with larger salaries to keep them in service or face a two-year wait until they could finally leave due to staffing issues. Luckily, my trade was overmanned, and my waiting time would be between six months and a year. It was autumn 2016, and I would be relieved of my military burden by August that next year.

I was called into the CO's office, a man I had much respect for, and we talked casually about my withdrawal. I listed the issues I had with the system, the job and the government. I also included my personal philosophies regarding the time we have on this planet, the love we must cherish within each of us, and my rejection towards the idea that non-issue black socks could be attributed to poor work ethic! He gave me the weekend to make sure my mind was made, but we both knew I had made my decision. For months I had hesitated and debated whether I should leave or not, considering my employability after service and future aspects I would benefit from if I did stay in the military. My biggest concern was what my family, especially my father, would have thought about me leaving a supposedly noble and wholesome profession I had wanted to be part of since a very young age. As I left the building that evening and headed towards my weekend, an enormous weight lifted from my shoulders as I knew by the end of next summer, I would no longer be physically and mentally restrained by the military, and my personal feelings regarding conflict amongst humanity would no longer interfere with my conscious.

***

Sometime in 2016, Tom and my mother's business had failed. With her influence in their business dissolved, it's difficult to ascertain exactly what happened. Though I still hadn't established contact with her any more than a hand full of well-wishing text messages, I did manage to visit her again one time with my sister, but we barely lasted an hour before both being shut down by her mean ways. As we left, I told my sister that I really didn't think that she had much longer to live. Shortly after this visit, I received a call from the same sister with the definitive results from the hospital that was trying to find out why her condition was deteriorating quickly. To our upset, we found out that she had developed Motor Neurone Disease, otherwise known as MND, or ALS in the United States, the same condition physicist Steven Hawking's eventually died of, though his longevity was very uncommon. Most patients have around three years of life until they pass away, but as the symptoms of her stroke had masked the MND, doctors were unsure how long she would survive for. She had a particular type of the disease which first acted on the throat and mouth, paralysing her speech and her ability to swallow. She had been living on breakfast drinks for some time leading up to the diagnosis, and her mouth hung shallowly, with her lips drooping at the corner. She dribbled frequently, and often choked on her drink, spitting it over herself often. While at the moment this was the most obvious of symptoms, her mobility had almost dropped to nothing as the disease wasted away her functions. Due to her inability to eat healthily, she had become just skin and bone. I do not regret our history or my decision to back away from her, I only regret the events I could have handled better that led to my decision not to see her often as she eventually began to lose her grasp on life.

December 2016, Christmas leave was approaching quickly (what is it with drama at Christmas?) It was a few weeks before my leave was to start when I received a call from an unknown number. I answered and heard a rather sullen sounding Tom who informed me that the doctors had discovered that my mother, who was now living in the hospital, was a few days away from dying. She had contracted pneumonia and couldn't summon the strength to cough or breathe through the illness and was sure to pass away within days. I told my sergeant of the issue and was granted just under a month's leave as well as any compassionate leave I needed, so I set off with Bandit that evening in my small pickup truck towards Ipswich hospital. Fairy lights from the houses gleamed in festive neon brightness, while children and their parents held hands through warm, woolly mittens as they walked along the damp pavement. Homely light poured from the windows of the houses as families prepared their final shopping lists for Christmas dinner that was just days away. Like Chris Rae's 'Driving home for Christmas', red lights of cars stuck in traffic were all around, and a wet, wintery English mist drenched the windscreen of my truck. The invisible, intangible excitement of a nation preparing for presents, love and joy to the world seemed omnipresent. Though the atmosphere of Christmas was alive, my heart, the only aperture that Christmas is truly experienced through, was cold as I knew my mother's death was approaching. I drove silently to the carpark, set Bandit food and water, and made my way through the maze of the clinically clean white-washed hospital wards. The walls swelled and towered over me, just like the scenes from my nightmares and flashbacks, and I fought the desire to panic or cut myself. I had knowingly walked into the jaws of my worst dreams, and had to open up tightly stitched wounds just so I could muster one last loving, vulnerable moment with my dying mother. I found her ward, pushed open the swinging doors and united myself with both my sisters at the foot of our mum's hospital bed.

She was skeletal and semi-conscious. Her breathing was laboured and weak. She would occasionally try and cough, but her inability to do so meant she had to try and swallow to clear her throat. There was a viscus, syrup-like water that she would drink to soothe her pains, but she was so skinny and weak she could barely hold the cup. She had all kinds of tubes coming in and out of her, and lots of bruises all over from where needles had

185

previously administered drugs. Her skin was always beautifully tanned as she spent so much time outside caring for her garden, but her once youthful, healthy skin sagged around her bones with a yellowish tint. We each spent time alone with her, holding her hand and telling her of our love for her. I saw so much pain in her eyes, and she weakly touched my hand as her only response to the loving things I was saying. She cried and forced a cough to clear the emotions that built up in her throat. While I was with her, she must have dipped in and out of unconsciousness a few times. It was then that, understanding how life is only wonderful because we know how limiting it is, and death was only so painful because how unknown that next chapter is, I told her that if she wanted to let go, she could. She didn't have to suffer any longer, we all understood what was happening, and what needed to happen in order to end her suffering. She looked at me, and half-smiled, and I returned the same gesture. I held my mum one last time, certain that the next few hours would be her last. My sisters and I gathered together before leaving and a doctor told us that she had just a 1% chance of making it through the night. At that moment, a nurse we will call Willy Wonker, came and interrupted the gloomy scene by asking her which flavour yoghurt she would like, chocolate or strawberry! The strange interruption broke up the mood, we accepted the doctor's verdict and wished our mother well on her final voyage. Speaking so candidly of it now seems strange, but the hospital had already allowed us to see her well past the visiting hours, and other patients were in the ward, restricting us from staying the night by her side.

The next morning, expecting to hear she had passed away in the night, we turned up to the hospital to find her condition had miraculously improved. In fact, the days leading up to Christmas saw her improve so

186

much that she had entirely fought off her symptoms by Christmas day. Though it was wonderful that she had survived, we knew that she wouldn't have much longer left as pneumonia had weakened her further and if she did live much longer, what condition would she be in? She already couldn't walk, struggled to breathe and had to be fed directly through a tube into her stomach. She hated her life when she was just about able to walk with a stick, so living like this would have been unbearably miserable for her. With her life prolonged, her suffering would intensify over the following weeks and I had a new pitiful experience to deal with – wanting your own mother to die so that her suffering would end. The wound I reopened to allow the love I gave to her to flow In and out became infected with my confused desire for her death. I wished her not to suffer anymore, but the only way that was possible was for her to pass away. She survived the 1% chance that she was given, and now she would die slowly as her organs began to fade away. My old friend self-harm crept up on me through my new confusion, eventually causing me to spend endless hours in my barrack room alone with a cold, blunt blade stuck into my arm.

***

I returned to the airbase after Christmas, and my responsibilities continued the same as they had done before. One evening after work, I got back into my tiny room, took off my uniform and also removed the happy face I put on to show my colleagues that I was fine, nothing to worry about. Instantly, I fell to the floor crippled by my overwhelming hopelessness. I had wanted to cut my arm all day, as this day in particular was hard for some reason. Some of you may understand that depression seems to come in waves, and this was a big one. I fell on the carpet, drew the knife across my arm, then pressed it hard into the flesh between my thumb and index finger. The pain washed away some of the sufferings, but today, for the first time, the pain I wanted to feel wasn't enough. My only coping mechanism, a bad habit that I had once conquered but had approved again, had gripped me, but this time it had failed to help me cope. I knew that suicide would be my only immediate way out. Through my tears and pain, I felt a tiny, painful tugging at my hair. Bandit the ferret had heard me come home, woke up and slithered his furry, cat like (but also remarkably snake like) body out of his cage and towards me laying broken on the floor. He had rustled through my hair, grabbed a thick strand and pulled hard from the root, working the hairs through his teeth! I instantly lit up happily, knowing that, through all the miles of driving between hospital visits and RAF bases, Bandit was beside me all along. In the lonely hours away from friends, family, Samantha and her wonderful home, Bandit was the only constant companion and the only living creature who saw me in my most vulnerable of states. He dug and nibbled at my ears, making me laugh loudly as he tickled me. He stuck his fuzzy, pointy face into my ear and with a big *sniff-sniff-SNIFF* sent shivers down my spine. Goosebumps turned my arms into mountain ranges, and I exploded with laughter. I picked up the little rascal under his shoulders and he gave me a cheeky look as his flexible body and legs hung loosely. He may have just been annoying me because he wanted food, but he came to my side right at the perfect moment (I like to think it was more than just a good time for him to ask me for dinner.) Bandit was more than just an adventurous pet, as he had just taken his first steps to become one of the only beings on Earth who kept me alive. On these two occasions that I would like to share, just the thought of Bandit alone kept me from ending my life.

I clocked off from my day's labour around 1730, it was a day that I was experiencing another extremely depressive low. I heard on the radio about a man in Peterborough who had climbed the other side of a bridge over a motorway and was finding his peace before he would jump. The news, coupled with my own longing to end my life that evening, inspired me to find a similar bridge, and wish farewell to suffering. I drove out towards the coast, parked my car on the road, then walked across some fields and found a bridge that I knew would be high enough to end my life cleanly, without failure or fatally wounding me before shock finished me off. The sun was hanging low in the sky, setting the small tufts of grass and leafless shrubs in the field alive in a golden blaze. My heart was heavy, but the short countryside walk from my car was lovely, and In the middle distance I could see the bridge that would be my suicide spot. Unlike before, I no longer cared about having a non-violent end, I just wanted the suffering to cease. As I walked, I projected images of my family in my head, especially my mother in her failing condition. Strangely, the love I felt for her made me feel even more intoxicated that my departure from life would somehow make her passing easier for her, as perhaps we could both meet in the life after this one. I ran my hands over the cold bicycle restriction barrier that was positioned at either end of the bridge and instinctively looked down to my heal as if to manage Bandit's lead around the metal fence like I had done one hundred times before on our previous adventures across the country. I had just finished work, so I knew Bandit was still in my barracks tucked up asleep waiting for me to come home and give him a treat. It was at that moment I was struck by the realisation of who was going to look after Bandit. Who would give him the walks he needed? Would there be someone who could love him and feed him like I did? I couldn't bear the thought of Bandit returning to the rescue centre and loosing what I told him would be his forever home with me. Instantly I knew I had to rethink my death. I needed a plan of how I was going to do this with minimal casualties, just ending my life and upsetting nobody else's harmony, especially Bandits.

I walked up to the bridge, gripped the rusty steel beams and lifted myself onto the first tier of the short metal barrier. Empty crisp packets and plastic bottles rattled down the footpath over the bridge as the wind blew light and cold. The traffic below was an endless stream of noise and motion. If I had jumped, many people who would never know my name or why I had taken my life would be scarred forever by my bent and broken corpse. I may have even caused a car accident too, or cause others to kill themselves over witnessing such a tragic affair. I lifted my head, took a step backward towards solid ground, an breathed in the evening air. I had set out that evening to jump, but thankfully was saved by just the thought of that little ferret. A swell of sudden contemplation opened my mind as I saw every action had a consequence, and every thought, that initial spark of happiness or sadness that makes us human, could serve us limitless harm or unending fulfilment depending on how we used those thoughts.

On another occasion, I was working nights when madness visited me again and crashed through my brain like a tsunami. When the wave hit me, I was driving a small work van in rural Lincolnshire in the dead of night. Usually, I would wait until I got home and cut myself to relieve my tension,

190

but this method had stopped assisting me long ago. Knowing that would be no good, I gripped the steering wheel and with angry, tearful eyes, screamed loudly my frustration to a god that wanted to silently test my constitution to breaking point. The part of the road I found myself on was very straight, but there was a bend about half a mile away which was heavy with trees either side of the tarmac. Time was approaching midnight and it was a weekday, so I was confident no vehicles were approaching around the corner and no others were behind me. I floored the accelerator and quickly approached 60mph. I unbuckled my seatbelt. 70mph and I closed my eyes. Still accelerating, the trees on the bend must have been just under one hundred meters away from my appointment with death when again, thoughts of Bandit and his stupid little face filled my mind – I was working nights and had totally forgotten to feed him! My eyes snapped open, and I broke firmly and skidded wildly through the corner, side to side across the single carriageway, giving a sharp *gggrrrr* as the ABS kicked in. The van snaked to a screeching halt, and my heart pounded heavily while tears blurred my vision. I looked in the rearview mirror, only my bright red brake lights illuminated the dark trees behind me. I had clearly skidded well past the point I was aiming at and by luck alone kept the vehicle on the road without any damage. I collected my thoughts, straightened the vehicle and realised that again, Bandit had unknowingly saved my life. He never did rescue me from a burning building or perform CPR on me (if you have a good imagination that's a really funny thing to think about), but in his own way, just the thought of his needs was enough to save my life that night. Just by simply existing in his own annoying, adorable and memorable self, he kept me alive.

***

The last time I saw my mother was in February 2017. I was part of a team of airmen assigned to manage the comings and goings of the military court based at the Colchester Garrison. She was in a hospital a short distance away, so despite my decision for us to not see each other to avoid further conflict with her or Tom, I allowed myself this one time to break the difficult rule I set myself. I finished work in the early evening and ran to Colchester train station, hopped on the train, and made the short journey to Ipswich. When I arrived at the hospital, visiting hours had finished, though as I often found with all my hospital visits over the last few years, the ward nurses would always allow me to see her, they knew her condition was terminal. She sat upright in her bed, one hand in a bony death lock, the other clutching her phone. She was so happy to see me, and her face lit up like a child at a surprise birthday party. We hugged, and I sat beside her as she typed what she wanted to say on a neat bit of equipment that spoke aloud the things that had been typed. By this time, she had almost completely lost the function of her throat and mouth muscles. After a while the dull voice of the built-in software became annoying, and my mother clearly was displeased with the robotic lady, throwing her to the foot of the bed. We spent the next forty minutes chatting about all the funny, lighter aspects that her condition had brought.

When she first had her stroke, she had lost the politeness filter that allows us to be patient, to be kind, to say please and thank you, and to not allow the inner bigoted old person that resides somewhere in all of us to emerge. On many occasions, we had to apologise to nurses and doctors who were told by her that they were not doing their job properly, or how some of them needed to find new careers altogether. Strangely, with the partial loss of her speech in the early days of her illness, she had also lost the ability to sing. Every time she tried, she ended up making up a completely new language and sang the strange words along to famously familiar songs. I played with her hospital bed controls, making her go up and down, and almost bend in half. We laughed hard together, and our happy time there alone in that ward past visitor hours was only broken by her occasional laboured cough. I told her how much I loved her, and that none of the past mattered anymore, though inside I knew to me it meant a great deal, I hadn't yet let go of our history.

I knew this would be the last time I would see her, and I wanted it to be a pleasant, happy memory, as happy as it can be beside your dying parent. She leaned forward to kiss me, but only managed to move her head an inch towards my face, so I moved in towards her and received my last kiss. I rested my head on her frail, skinny chest, and felt her good hand play on my hair, just the same way she did when I was a little boy. I hugged her tightly, barely feeling the pulse in her heart, and truly experienced how it felt to be beside a person with just a few days of life left within them. I stood, told her to be good and not cause too much mischief with the nurses, and walked what felt like a thousand miles between her bed and the door leading out of the ward. I looked over my shoulder and blew her a goodbye kiss. The last image I have of my mother is her, sat upright against the raised hospital bed, with the same brown eyes I too inherited staring back at me, half-smiling through her paralysis and painful knowing that this would be the last time we would see each other. I had the same knowing expression that this was a final farewell, and we were leaving not in the turmoil of an argument, or as two people hurt by the wickedness of an indifferent world, but as two friends once again. Our souls shared a powerful union once more as we both reached out to one another, but soon, one soul would be leaving as it was called to return to a realm beyond human comprehension. Where one's soul originates, so does it return to when its time here is complete.

***

March made itself at home as the warmer weather started to emerge, and so to did more wild adventures in the great outdoors with Bandit. My RAF career was approaching an end, as from May I would have leave until August, when I would start my civilian life all over again. Before my time was up, I had further Bushcraft courses to run as an instructor within the RAF, a Swedish canoe expedition and a two-week civilian Bushcraft course. My plan was to cram as much Bushcraft into these last days of military service as possible in order to pursue my dream of teaching people about the outdoors. It seemed through all the events in my life, nature had become my companion. Long walks in the country always seemed to settle my nerves, and I found solidarity during sunsets, watching a tide go in and out, striving towards a mountain top or paddling gently through river systems. So profound was my harmony during the times that I spent chopping wood in the gentle rain or sleeping in sub-zero temperatures in shelters made from tree branches that I struggled to see how a life filled with anything other than the bare essentials could add any more value at all to feeling more alive. In my up and down depressive states, suicide was a constant thought as I struggled to accept the situations I found myself in and I fought to keep up my happy appearance. In the woods, however, with limited food, comfort, and warmth, life could be found so freely existing by simply relying on one another.

The squirrel needed the acorn to survive just as much as the oak needed the squirrel to hide an acorn away, forget where it was placed, and just like that, another oak tree comes to life. The carpenter bee, a host in woody trunks of aged or dead trees, allows the life of other trees and plants to continue from their never-ending pollination. Our human existence is supported by the food we grow, owed to a six-inch layer of fertile soil and sporadic rains that the worlds farmers count on for the feeding of humanity. My place in the woods was determined not by what I thought of it, but by how it thought of me. If I was to sleep under an old tree, and in the night it fell and crushed me, maybe some people would cry and their lives pause for some time, but the woods wouldn't mourn my demise, only recycle my blood, grow on my flesh and sustain an endless chain of creatures who too would one day become part of something else's nutrition.

Never have I wanted to kill for pleasure or have killed for demonstration. While I agree with a more vegetarian existence while in nature, if animals such as deer, rabbits or pigeons have been killed as part of a cull, they can be used to fulfil an incredible purpose and teach others how to survive in a survival scenario or simply to have a better understanding of the life our ancestors once had. When preparing food, I always found it vitally important to say a silent prayer to the animal or sometimes even plant, to thank them for the usage I or my group would get from them. It is always a blessing to be involved in understanding the universe, god or *the way* through nature. When I found my physical body suspended in nature, I felt my heart lifted to a higher purpose amongst the clouds with the birds, or in the roots of the trees deep beneath my feet. The modern world with all its noise, rushing, judgements and so on was not a place I felt I could heal myself and protect my own nature, and for good reason too. While humankind tries to dominate the planet, we have found that our very doing so has poisoned our oceans with chemicals, our air with toxins, and stripped the Earth away of its natural beauty to fuel our ceaseless march to the cry of more! More! More! – and in that process, we have suffocated ourselves. So, breathe fresh air regularly and isolate yourself from the modern world for some time every day by appreciating nature. Listen to the birds singing their life stories for no cost at all, and marvel at the stars, the most beautiful thing we can see on Earth. As far as we know, we are the only being that has looked up at night and seen a shooting star, and thought just how lovely that thing is - and how small our own existence is compared to everything else! To summarise my brief feelings towards nature and our place amongst it, I believe the problem with man isn't that we don't see enough sunsets, but that we don't sit and watch long enough to see the stars come out and wonder at the mysterious beauty of it all - a beauty we are a part of.

Late one afternoon in March I received a troubling text message from my uncle. Tom had arranged for him and my mother to be married from her bed in a hospice she was moved to so she could live out her last days in a warm, friendly environment. A church official was present with a celebrant who would marry her and Tom together, but they had refused to allow the wedding to take place as when asked if her family had been told about the wedding, Tom reacted angrily, telling them that no other family members should know about their plans. One of the hospice nurses told the celebrant that their patient had three children, and so the marriage was postponed until we had all been informed about the union. I was shocked to discover the audacity of Tom. Once again, I had underestimated him, and he had walked all over me, my family and most importantly my dying mother. I found out more details of this occurrence late in the evening when I called the personal out of hours contact number of the chaplin. She gave me the details when I struck up a conversation with her once during a visit to the hospital church. I called her and introduced myself as the son of the woman who she was due to marry that day, and we had met at the church before then. She told me how it was unlike any other bedside wedding she had attended. My mother wasn't dressed, wasn't wearing any makeup and her hair was in a mess, she hadn't even been washed that day! The only people in attendance were Tom and his brother. They knew something wasn't right, and when they questioned the unusual circumstances, Tom became aggressive towards them. My mother was asked privately if she wanted her children to know about the wedding, and she agreed that we should know. Now we all had been informed, the wedding was due to take place the very next day.

I told her my mother wasn't in a stable mindset, and Tom, though he dutifully cared for her, had other relationships and had done so for a while. I explained the past abuse that he had bestowed on her and his cruel treatment of others. I thought that surely it must be impossible to marry the two, she could barely even speak! The chaplin told me there was nothing she could do, the wedding had to take place, and unless my mother changed her mind, the two would be married by tomorrow afternoon. What I had told her, however, would weigh heavily on the side of the marriage being postponed again if they found her in a similar state. Even in her final days, Tom's wicked way was testing her and our family in a whole new degree.

I got home from my late shift at mid-evening, played with Bandit to occupy my mind so that I wouldn't be tempted into self-harm, then made my way to the kitchen. I prepared my vegetables, and while they were boiling, adjusted my suicide note once more, to be a more fitting, exact account as to why I was leaving and how my suicide wasn't a cry for help but a final way of controlling my own life, forbidding anyone else to tamper with my happiness once and for all. Having completed the first step towards checking out, I put away the note, this time saving a digital copy in my mobile phone too, then began serving my meal which I intended to be my last. My phone buzzed again in my pocket and I tutted as it always seemed somebody wanted to call me right when I was about to eat my dinner, watch a film, or like that night, kill myself. I put down the serving spoon and fished through my pocket to answer the call. The number was unrecognised, but from my memory I knew exactly who the caller was. My stomach rolled and became an empty pit, while my heart raced up from my throat all the way to my mouth. I closed my eyes, breathed in calmly and swiped across the green icon on the screen.

"Charlie? It's Tom."

I clenched my jaw and fist, preparing for an argument. It felt as if I was the only one standing in his way. I was the unwanted teenage son. It was because of me standing up for myself that we had the fight three years before. He once came home to an empty house and my mother missing without knowing where she was largely due to me. Now again it was me who had stepped in front of his unknown motivation to marry her, and I made it clear I did not think it was ethical for anyone with a history like theirs to be considering marriage. I said hello and awaited what I thought would be an incoming barrage of insults, figuring he had discovered my conversation with the chaplain. But I was wrong.

"Your mum has just passed away."

***

The following morning I arose early and packed Bandit into my car for another voyage down south. The traffic was awful, and I arrived at the hospice much later than I had expected. I had gone to collect documents and personal belongings, which was the job of my eldest sister as she was her next of kin, but she was on holiday when we received the call, so I had taken the responsibility. Though I had gone to speak with the hospice officials and understand the details of her passing, I knew I would be meeting Tom and my mother's immediate family, the same people who had always taken Tom's lies for the truth.

I parked my car outside the peaceful but busy hospice, surrounded by trees, beautiful architecture and softly coloured brickwork and flagstones. Walking into the building, I was pleasantly surprised to see so many drawings, hanging art, colourful posters and bright decorations. I signed in, wore my visitors badge, and was escorted by a nurse through a clean corridor lined with windows that let in beautiful daylight. The nurse stopped at a door, knocked softly, twisted the handle and entered, gesturing me to take my place inside the family room. I thanked her, and she turned and left. The room I entered was very dark, only dimly lit by a few small lampshades in the corners of the enclosed space. Decorations seemed to festoon the walls like the rest of the hospice, but the light was too dim to pick out what colours they were, or indeed what they displayed at all. Six figures sat in a semi-circle facing a senior member of the family care team. Instantly, I noticed my mother's brother rise from the darkness and embrace me. It was the first I had seen my uncle in a very long time, and though I felt a warm, loving energy coming from his side of the room and indeed the hug itself, the other figures remained seated and cold. The next person to introduce herself was the senior nurse. Again, she warmly embraced me and smiled so lovingly she instantly put my mind to rest. I was now in the middle of the horseshoe of chairs and turned to see Tom's figure next to raise from the seats. He held out his hand to shake mine, and without hesitation, I took it and embraced him. While the history between us was turbulent, the human being stood before me needed love and affection like any other being in mourning deserves. He had been the master of my misery, and along with my mother, the monster of my suicidal condition, but I refused to be a reflection of someone else's evil, and I chose instead to give him what was at the core of my essence – love. I greeted the other members in the room, but after having believed the lies bestowed upon them, one person refused to even lift their head to acknowledge me after all this time, even when faced with the same tragic circumstance we shared in common.

I sat for half an hour listening to how my mother had died, and how comfortable she was in her final moments. We each chipped into the conversation, adding what we thought was a good contribution to the unexpected eulogy. Though at the time suicide was a constant thought in my mind, having even made plans the night before her death to also meet my own, I never allowed myself to be seen by others as miserable and depressed. In fact, none of my family, my girlfriend or colleagues knew of my struggles, though some knew of my personal circumstances. We discover a great paradox when we learn that some of our societies most happy, accomplished individuals, are often the ones who also take their own lives. My attention as I write this is drawn to Robin Williams, Marilyn Monroe and most recently Chester Bennington of Linkin Park.

I looked around the room and saw the unpleasant misery on the faces of all the family members who had turned to despise me in support for Tom's campaign to smear my name. Though at the time I was holding back years of family upset, domestic struggle and postponed suicides, I was the only person in the room still able to hold a smile, look into the eyes of the nurse and say on behalf of everyone in her life, we could never thank the hospice staff enough for what you all did for her. I told the nurse that I knew how much hard work they put into supporting families and their unwell loved ones, and I couldn't have imagined a nicer place and people to be there for her last moments. The nurse smiled and thanked me for my words, when an influential family member spoke up from their miserable, listless state of melancholy, to look me in the eye for the first time in years and say "yes, thank you for being kind to all those who bothered to see her before she died", an obvious stab at my reluctancy to see her before she passed away. The words stung me at first, but I simply returned a smile, and decided to forgive them of their misunderstanding of me. In the process of realising they were just an easily manipulated individual, too set in their own bitter way to even begin to try to distinguish the truth from lies, I allowed myself to stay in my own peace and not sink to their lower level. Instead of judgment, I sent out love and accepted that person for who they were.

I looked around again at the morbid faces, as if they were all dramatically determined to show the world how miserable they were and how awful their lives are. While their sadness was a true feeling and everyone has a right to mourn in their own way, I instinctively found the calm, the good and the best in this situation. We had all lost someone we loved, but at the same time, her suffering had been let go. Who are we to mourn the loss of a person suffering in discomfort and pain, when that pain wasn't ours to begin with? She had her final liberation and while it was a sad affair to never see her again, the circle of life had been completed. Fear of death seemed so obscure to me. Worrying and being scared by the thought of what happens when we die, where do we go and what do we become all seemed like totally inappropriate questions. We don't ask where we were before we were born! It seems insane to think of these questions fearfully, as does it also seem mad to worry yourself to sickness with striving to acquire large quantities of material wealth, elevated social statuses or vain achievements. Eventually, the carrot becomes smaller than the stick, and the value of the items diminish under the weight of the stress you adopt while trying to achieve them.

Though I couldn't connect physically or mentally with the people in that room, I noticed that their faces didn't have to be a reflection of mine on

202

the outside. As my way always was, I made it my goal to be the most hopeful, cheery individual of a group when faced with hardship. Though I was externally positive, their external misery was exactly how I felt on the *inside* for over a year now. I refused to let anyone see the extreme unhappiness I waded through every day, only I was allowed to see that part and plot against myself to end my suffering. I realised just how hypocritical, dishonest and two faced towards myself I was being. Surely, if I could so quickly feel and intolerance towards other peoples miserable appearance, but accept them for who they were and only think peaceful thoughts towards them, then why wasn't I treating myself the same way? All I was doing was reliving and recycling the past feelings over and over again. I knew acting like this would only make me sicker, but I just couldn't let go of my feelings – I wanted to hold onto the depression! The past was far behind me, and with my mother now gone, there was no reason Tom would appear in my life again. It really was time to forgive myself, learn from this time, and become friends with myself again. It was time to take better care of myself.

At that moment, the past pain of betrayal, spite and anger were let go. The anger I reserved for them people was released. The hate I felt for the way I had been treated was forgotten. If I could be loving towards others even in the most unfair of times, then I could and should be loving to myself and choose to end the depression not because I wanted it to be gone, but because I didn't need to hold onto it at all! I felt so irregular and strange because of my new understanding that this whole time, it was purely my own thinking that had walked me down the path of depression. I was humbled by all the churning emotions inside from the lessons that flooded my way throughout the pain I had endured, events I had survived and characters that had tested me. As I let go of my history, I felt my constant suicidal thoughts lift away from my inner features, dissolve and finally reveal a fresh, pure version of myself. I had been forged in the heat of the scorn these people had given to me since I was 16, but I had come out stronger than before, with a new understanding of life through the death of my mother. The situation didn't define me, it revealed me, and the lessons I had been learning which came in different forms over the years were steadying my mind and spirit in that very moment, bringing me perfect balance. It is really true that when my mother said, "if you want something, you have to go and get it. Don't let anyone tell you what you can or you can't have." I had just started to believe for a better life for myself in that dark, depressing room, and just as I had no choice but to let my mother go, I let go of my suicide and all the baggage I had carried. It wasn't external forces that had torn my life apart, it was my own reaction to them, so I made a promise then that I would no longer be the hostage to my imagination and ego. The oneness that I had understood so well at the church many years ago had installed in me an ability to learn through pain, and each day I worked closer and closer to understanding a new lesson which would reveal my true nature. *The way* had shown me *my* way, and for the first time, I understood exactly why everything had happened.

I regretted nothing and gave no excuses for my failings. I accepted all my shortcomings and traded the bitterness I had accumulated from other people for love. My life flashed before my eyes, and on exiting the dark, dimly lit room, full of my past, present, physical and imagined demons, I stepped into the light of the corridor and wandered my way to the exit. As if being born again, I breathed deeply, looked up to the sky, and handed over my problems and bad feelings to the wind.

I let go, and let god.

Bandit was asleep in the back of the car, cozied up in his hammock under a pile of smelly blankets. He stirred, and seemed to eye me curiously as if he knew a shift had taken place inside of me. He sniffed at the air and peered at me under his fluffy mountain of bedding. We drove back to rural Essex in silence as I smiled softly to myself, remembering the best experiences with my mum over the years I knew and loved her, and everything this tale, now that it had a conclusion, had to teach me. I stopped outside Samantha's house, took Bandit out of the cage and slipped on his collar, clipping on the lead. The beautiful trees all around this area swayed as if welcoming home the person I was placed on Earth to be, their emerging leaves waving from within their opening buds on every tip of every twig and branch, cheering for my new found peace. A blackbird flew up from the grass and perched on a branch some meters above my head. Feeling easy with my presents, she sang her high-pitched song and stopped after just a few notes. I wondered if she was a messenger sent to ask me what I was going to do next?

***

I felt nature and the countryside calling me, after all, today the sky was clear with just a few fluffy clouds here and there, the perfect setting for an adventure with The Bandit. We walked together through the grassy fields some miles behind my old house. It was late winter in a rural area of Essex,

England. Mud clung to my boots, and Bandit was soggy from the dew that clung to the grass, but it wasn't much farther until I would reach my awaiting destination. It must have been just above freezing by this time in the afternoon, and the frozen crystals on each individual blade of grass reflected a myriad of colour across the tree-lined countryside. I was heading to St. Andrews church, a small, ancient church in a village not far from here. The vistas from on top of the hill that the church sat on were incredible, but the old English church had a beautiful allure too. The patina of the old stones and weathered wooden beams were the perfect place to take a seat and reflect, and the low hanging winter sun added a golden brilliance to the buildings sharp edges which stood in contrast with the hazy hues of a winter afternoon.

My backside came to a soft bump on the bench on the east side of the church, and I picked up the soggy, tired Bandit. Together we watched in silence as farm vehicles worked steadily miles away in silence, muffled by the acres of fields between us. In the middle distance, the drone of commuter traffic moved ceaselessly as people freely travelled about and tackled their daily tasks. A gentle wintry breeze chilled my face, firing blood vessels and ripening my cheeks rosy. Though this was the same location and roughly the same time that I had been here seven years before, I needed no sudden epiphanies to push my consciousness towards wholeness and inspiration. All of Gods teachings, Allah's prayers, or Krishna's mantras couldn't have inspired or taught me more than I had learned along the path of these last few years. While some of these events may not have been avoidable, I recognised then that my attitude towards these difficulties was my choosing, and from that day I would choose to live happily, without

206

anger, stress or conflict as freely as I possibly could, promising myself that I would react to life's ups and down's in the most harmonious way I knew possible.

An inconvenience is an adventure wrongly considered, and I was now ready to put that idea to the test. "Bandit," I said, looking down at my little buddy, who had curled himself up in my jacket, fast asleep in the warmth of my body heat, "Let's go for a long, long walk through the countryside. How does Hadrian's Wall sound? I think I've learned all I need to know before our adventures."

Charlie and The Bandit went on to raise thousands of pounds for the MND Association and other charities by starting the first of many fundraising events together, which include trekking across Hadrian's Wall, walking across historic military battle grounds in full period uniforms and skateboarding forty miles through London. In 2018, they said farewell to Samantha who passed away eleven months after his own mother. With a taste for adventure and understanding that his destiny is in his own hands, Charlie sold his belongings, left his job, bought a campervan and travelled 10,000 miles through Europe with Bandit in aid of the charity Save Our Soldier. The details of these events and the epic adventure from the Arctic Circle to Sicily will be published in his next book named after the duo's charitable organisation, 'Adventures With The Bandit'.

Being Human

Start all your adventures with limited knowledge. You will never know everything you think you need to before an undertaking. Sooner or later you must let go and surrender to the current of life that guides us to where we need to be - always choose sooner. Find the courage to face everything with curiosity and follow all roads far and wide with wonder in your heart. Be flexible, allow circumstances to come to you. Surrender gracefully when it's time for previous circumstances to leave. Move on. Sympathise with everyone, judge no one. Let calm be who you are, not something you are. Every event has come to help you grow, but don't expect to grow the same way each time. You are not alone, so find companionship and let someone else realise they aren't alone either. Fill your life with sunsets, laughter, stargazing and compassion – the best things in life are free. Listen to everything and everyone, but be silent yourself. Silence is the stitching that holds together the seams of life. Believe in your dream no matter how trivial it may seem and do one thing every day to keep that dream alive. Love in every way you can. Smile at a stranger. Give away something you like to someone who would like it more. Attach no conditions to your kindness. When everything else is gone, love will remind you that it can never leave. Love should not be retracted, and it can never be exchanged. Love for loving sake. Do your hearts work, not work that pays for a chosen lifestyle. Make your passion your lifestyle. If you seek revenge, dig two graves. Find gratitude for everything around you, and let the words "thank you, thank you, thank you" be your daily prayer. There is no greater time than right now, so remind yourself of your blessings, smile, and live every day in peace.

Acknowledgements

Bandit, words to express my ceaseless gratitude for our friendship escape me. I owe every breath I take to you. For tolerating hours of my silent contemplation, being a shoulder to cry on as I dug up old memories and for being my inspiration, I have to thank Chiara. Your unending love and support hold the pages of this book together. To my family, friends and followers, thank you for encouraging me to get part of this story into words. I'm endlessly grateful for the wisdom of my teachers Dr. Wayne Dyer and Alan Watts, I hope my readers embrace your words and use them to empower their lives too. I'm honoured to be using Amazon as a platform to launch new authors, this would have been a much more difficult process without their service. Kayley, who has designed every piece of artwork I've needed, you already know that not all heroes wear capes. Lastly, a huge round of applause to my editor, Becka, for my countless questions, hours of hard work editing my writing, and being an all round legend.

About the Author

Charles P. Hammerton is an award-winning fundraiser, speaker and teacher. When he's not writing in the small blue and white sailing boat he lives on with his other half in Cornwall, England; he's teaching children and adults how to enjoy the great outdoors through his bushcraft company, Adventure Bandits. Charlie first gained the attention of the public after his adventurous challenges and travel with his best friend, a ferret called Bandit. While Bandit is no longer with us, his spirit inspires Charlie to help people make the most of their life through inspirational speaking and writing.

To book Charlie for a speaking engagement or school visit, search CharlesHammerton.com online, or Adventures with Charles Hammerton on Facebook.

To book a day of Adventure Bandits bushcraft, visit AdventureBandits.co.uk, or search for Adventure Bandits on Facebook.

Printed in Great Britain
by Amazon

35483377R00132